Also by
Rachel Kauder Nalebuff

Stages: On Dying, Working, and Feeling

The Feminist Utopia Project
(coedited with Alexandra Brodsky)

My Little Red Book

Intimate Histories
of Periods, Growing,
and Changing

Our Red Book

GATHERED BY

Rachel Kauder Nalebuff

SIMON & SCHUSTER
New York   London   Toronto
Sydney   New Delhi

Simon & Schuster
1230 Avenue of the Americas
New York, NY 10020

First Simon & Schuster hardcover edition November 2022

SIMON & SCHUSTER and colophon are registered
trademarks of Simon & Schuster, Inc.

For information about special discounts for bulk purchases,
please contact Simon & Schuster Special Sales at
1-866-506-1949 or business@simonandschuster.com.

The Simon & Schuster Speakers Bureau can bring authors
to your live event. For more information or to book an
event, contact the Simon & Schuster Speakers Bureau at
1-866-248-3049 or visit our website at www.simonspeakers.com.

Interior design by Lewelin Polanco

Manufactured in the United States of America

1 3 5 7 9 10 8 6 4 2

Library of Congress Cataloging-in-Publication Data is available.

ISBN 978-1-9821-6865-0
ISBN 978-1-9821-6867-4 (ebook)

Contents

Contents

A Brief Interlude on Menstrual Justice (or, What Is Menstrual Justice?)

Contents

Back into the Flood: More Stories from Writers & Artists

Intimate Conversations

Contents

A Full Circle: More Stories from Home

A Note from the Editor

In between your hands are many voices, speaking their most intimate histories related to bleeding and menstruation. Together, they offer a glimpse of history as it lives under the skin and pulses through us.

This book is not a comprehensive collection of every story there is to tell about first blood, last blood, missing periods, birth, bleeding after transitioning, staining things, aching, grieving, communing, aging, and changing. Rather, it is a telling that has unfolded over my lifetime. It is a web of memories gathered from people I know, people they know—their parents, grandparents, friends, lovers—and eventually strangers I wanted to know—writers, experts, community leaders, activists, young people, and other visionaries.

Like periods, these histories are not tidy or neat. They trickle, overflow, and circle back. They can weigh you down, inspire sudden joy, and instill spirituality. These accounts are not what Americans might call "stuff for children," and yet, they are what children live through.

Some voices in this collection echo one another, and others rub against one another, forming a chorus that resembles reality. Each account stands on its own, but if you read pieces in order, you may find that patterns, connections, and fateful threads await your discovery.

As much as I can, I want to share these stories with you the way I would in person. Sometimes I'll tell you how a story came my way or how someone's story has altered me, haunted me, or led me down unexpected life paths. Given all the blood spilled, it seems important to speak with you from an intimate, human place.

The Aunts

I wonder what would have happened if I had understood shame as a young person. If this even could have been possible.

I'm only starting to understand it now. My friend Merkel explained it to me the other day while we were walking in the park.

"Underneath shame," she said, "is a source of power that someone is afraid of you unlocking."

And then she said, "I didn't come up with that. I heard it from a friend who's a witch, who also probably heard it first from someone else."

This book begins with a memory I received when I was a child.

I was twelve and shy.

I had recently gotten my first period while on vacation visiting my widowed grandfather. Despite my repeated calls home, no one in my family was picking up the phone. I cried, helplessly, in my grandfather's bathroom, holding an assortment of large tampons that must have been left behind by his deceased second wife.

Eventually, my grandfather drove me to a pharmacy, where he dropped me off in the parking lot and said, "Go inside and figure it out."

A few weeks later, at a family Passover seder in Queens, I was sitting at the kids' table, like every other year of my life beforehand. Clinking her glass, my mom announced to my extended family that I had "become a woman."

Looking back on it, I understand this moment and the day of my first period as my first of many encounters with shame. Though I also know that memory is slippery and that this is an attempt now, at age thirty, to make sense of a heat and weight I felt in my body then, for which I did not have words.

My tante Nina, my great-aunt, must have recognized something in me. Later that night, in her bedroom, which smelled like cat litter and everyone's winter coats piled onto the bed, she told me a story.

Tante Nina

I was thirteen. It was 1940. We were fleeing Poland and the deportation of the Jews. The atrocities committed by the Germans were getting worse. Ghettos were being formed. My uncles in Belgium and France went through enormous troubles to obtain visas and passage for us to get out. To reach Belgium, we had to pass through Germany. My story takes place on the train arriving from Poland at the German border crossing. The train stopped, and we were told to get completely undressed for the customs guards to search us.

The guards were mostly searching for hidden jewelry, and they looked in the most private places. It was horrible. I had hidden my yellow Star of David in my shoe, but it was discovered. In my fright, I completely lost it and peed in my pants. But when I looked down, what I saw was actually a stream of red. I raced into the compartment, and my mother saw what was happening. She rushed to the toilets at the end of the train and grabbed lots of rolls of toilet paper, one of which she shoved into my underwear. She was somehow able to do this so discreetly that my two sisters and brother never knew about this. She whispered to me that now I was going to be a big girl on whom she was going to have to depend, that this would happen every month. But most important, she told me, in Belgium and France, where we were heading, they had excellent napkins, much better than in Poland.

My great-aunt was tiny, with a large beak of a nose. She spoke with a thick French accent, and her voice was extremely nasal. Up until that point, our conversations had pertained mostly to making jewelry out of Sculpey and how much we both loved frozen waffles.

I knew she had lived through something. I knew she had fled "the war." But even words like *survive* and *Holocaust* felt abstract to me, as a child who had lived through nothing. For the first time, I saw my tante Nina as someone who had once been my age.

You lived through that?

My mother and my aunts had never heard this story, either.

"So your period spared you from being examined by the officer?" my mother asked.

"*Oui*," my tante Nina said. The officer had been too disgusted to continue.

"Why have you never shared this story *avec nous*?" my mom asked. "This story about your period saving your life."

"*Parce que ce n'est pas quelque chose à discuter.*"

Because it's not a subject we talk about.

My mom was shocked.

And yet, I had never heard my mother's first period story, either.

No one, of any generation, it seemed, had shared anything in any direction.

It was only after my great-aunt shared her story that my other family members started talking.

Aunt Lienna

I was in the hospital for a tonsillectomy. I was not quite eleven, and in Soviet Russia, if you were not yet a teenager, they would put you in a room with ten other kids.

They had a wooden armchair, similar to an execution chair, with all these straps. They strap your legs, your arms, and your body, and a nurse is holding your head, because there is only local anesthesia.

At the same time, another surgery is happening across the room. So you *see* what's happening—or about to happen—right in front of you. The other surgeon's apron is splattered with blood, and of course everyone is screaming.

The surgery was such a shock to my body, I think, that I got my period. There were no antibiotics, so hospitals, afraid of bacteria, would not allow parents to visit. But I was fortunate because my mom had already told me about periods.

Bleeding from my mouth and my vagina, I went to the nurse. I said, "I have my period. Can you give me something?" And then *she* started freaking out, and said, "Don't worry!!! It happens to EVERY WOMAN!!!" She was concerned I would lose too much blood. And also because I was so young.

At my age, there were few girls who had had their period. So there was no one to share it with. And then there was the extra hurdle that rooms were not separated by gender. But in a way, I think we were freer with bodies in Soviet Russia. We would run around naked, we would go swimming in just our underwear. Whereas here, girls cover their chests even before they have breasts.

When I was older and had fibroids, I would bleed so heavily that I would leave trails of blood on the floor or furniture. During menopause, I felt flashes of anxiety. A relentless wave, several times a day, sometimes at night. It's exhausting. Even your heart gets exhausted. To cope, I would visualize surfing. I knew it would roll in and back out. I would have conversations where people were talking to me and I was not paying attention at all. I was just focused on surfing.

I know this sounds incomprehensible. But women didn't talk about menopause because they were afraid to seem old. I had a friend in Russia who told me how women lied to their husbands. They'd put a little piece of liver in their underwear so that their husbands thought they still had their period and wouldn't think of them as old.

Little Aunt Nina
(named after Tante Nina)

I didn't have a mother in the traditional sense. What I had was a woman who knew she was dying. Who knew she would not be around to raise two little girls. My mom died when I was twelve and a half, and I got my period sometime that year.

Your grandmother and grandfather had a horrible history behind them of surviving the Holocaust, but when they had their children, they did not think about anything going wrong.

I know nothing of my mother's period story, and that's a shame. I just know that by the time it came close for me, she was already incapacitated by her disease. She also had enough neurosis left over from the war that she never felt like someone I could talk to.

That said, I *did* have an older sister who experienced everything before me. And I was no dope. When she wasn't around, I would go snooping in her room. I found cigarettes, and so I started smoking. I also found tampons. It wasn't like you, with your grandfather in CVS who just threw you into the ocean and said, "Go in there. Go figure it out." I had an older sister who had already figured it out. I don't know if she ever went into her cigarette carton or tampon box and said, "Huh, I wonder why five are missing!" I learned a lot just by playing with them, popping them out of their wrappers, wondering, *Huh, where does this go?*

There was a book on the bookshelf in your mom's room that filled in a lot of gaps between not having had sex ed or a mother: *Our Bodies, Ourselves.* I taught myself by looking through all the pages and holding up a mirror. I also read a book called *Are You There God? It's Me, Margaret.*

There's a passage in *Are You There God?* where the protagonist has this chant to develop breasts, and I did it *incessantly.* I'm the only one in our family blessed by the breast fairy . . . so maybe that stupid chant worked.

When my period came, I didn't know, because it wasn't red. I thought, *Did I shit in my pants?* Nowhere did I read it could be brown, it could be thick, it could be thin, it could be ropy.

I didn't live through any ritual. I lived through wanting to hurry it all up. I wanted the keys to the kingdom. I wanted to be done with the teenage years.

After I'd heard various family stories, my mom said, "Rachel, you are hearing stories that have never been told. By writing them down, you are doing something important. You are correcting an erasure in our histories.

"We should create a local archive of stories about menstruation," she proposed. "And we can even ask community leaders to participate!" This seemed very daunting to me at age fourteen, but I agreed.

My mother rarely expressed her feelings, so when she did, I took note. Her convictions formed my worldview and I believed whatever she believed.

She was also extremely organized. She had a room full of newspaper clippings and sheet music that she kept in labeled boxes. Over the years, she asked various friends about their first period stories, which she either transcribed or helped edit and then diligently put in the right drawer.

These are a few stories that were shared with my mom, and then shared with me, which shaped my sense of the many people in our small city.

A Small City: Stories from Home

Zannette

My first memory of my big day is marked by my dad's congratulations on my passage into womanhood. My mother had told him about the arrival of my period, just as she had done for my older sister two years earlier. I remembered my sister's disgust that my mother needed to share this event with my dad. In this summer of my twelfth year, I was experiencing that same feeling of being exposed and having more responsibility for myself. I nevertheless had a lot of good feelings because my mom had prepared me for this arrival.

Although my mother was a librarian by training, at the time of my first period, she was a stay-at-home mom. During my growing-up years, my mom practiced her library skills, such as her love of reading and the sharing of information, with her family and many of my friends. She gave my sister and me loads of books about menstruation, coming of age, female sexuality, and emotions years before our big day. Many of our friends would come over to our house to talk with my mom about their big day and growing-up issues. My friends felt uncomfortable discussing these topics with their own moms and knew we had a lot of information on the subject. She would always tell them to let their moms know that we were having these chats and that, if a mother considered this information inappropriate for her daughter to hear, she should let my mother know. Our friends' moms saw my mother as a credible and supportive resource and found it okay that she was having these chats with their daughters.

She would tell us stories of how Black women came of age during the Depression and earlier in Virginia. She was brought up by her grandmother, who was born and reared in an enslaved African family in Virginia. Grandma was a young girl when her family was emancipated. My mother described how Black women used cloths during this early time because disposable sanitary napkins were not readily available. Women had to go through a painstaking process to take care of themselves during their monthly periods. My mother also relayed stories from her grandmother about Black women who had their first periods in Virginia during slavery. When these girls got their first period, it meant that they were now able to breed and suckle for their masters. It also meant that the young women lost the responsibility for their own bodies, feelings, and futures. Once these young women had their first period, they were often sold away from their families because they had become more valuable to their owners. The girls could be sold or hired out to other plantations for breeding or suckling duties. With the arrival of their first period, many of these young women were initially bred with their masters, members of his family, or other slaves on the plantation before they were hired out or sold to another plantation.

My mother always made us aware that as Black girls, our first period was one of the most significant events in our lives. We were now capable of becoming mothers and needed to become more responsible for our bodies, our feelings, and, in many ways, our futures.

On my big day, when my dad arrived with his well wishes, I was prepared for receiving them on many levels, though not for such a deep feeling of personal change. I knew when Dad congratulated me that I was no longer his little girl but a young woman. The carefree sense about myself, my body, and my life was over, and now I was responsible.

Zannette Eloise Lewis was a dynamic source of wisdom and a beacon of inspiration for the many communities she steadfastly served during her too-short life. Organizations that greatly benefited from her leadership include the Arts Council of Greater New Haven, Astrological Society of Connecticut, Inc., Connecticut Office of Higher Education, Episcopal Diocese of Connecticut, National Council of Negro Women, New Haven Museum and Historical Society, New Haven (CT) Chapter of The Links, Inc., and Yale Peabody Museum of Natural History. More than a decade after her passing, Zannette's spiritual light continues to shine over Connecticut and beyond.

A few years after she wrote this story, Zannette's story was read aloud by her family at her funeral.

Kica

My story begins about five years before I got my actual period. We had moved from Puerto Rico to Trinidad and were living in an apartment until we could find a house to live in. I remember one day picking up a piece of red candy from a bowl, popping it into my mouth, and sucking on it for a while. I didn't like it, and since I was in the bathroom at the time, I simply threw the candy into the commode and flushed. Several hours later, my mother yelled for all of us girls (I am the youngest of four siblings; three of us are female) to come to the bathroom—*immediately*. She started grilling us about who had used the bathroom last, whether any of us were sick or bleeding, and whether any of us had gotten our period. We all denied it and asked her why. She finally showed us the water in the bowl; it was bright red. I then realized that the culprit was the candy and told her. The relief on her face was immediately apparent, and we all started laughing. She used the opportunity to explain to us yet again about periods. We already knew a bit, as we'd asked about the giant boxes of sanitary napkins prominently displayed in her bathroom.

In Latino culture, getting your period is a significant event, a time when you become a *señorita*. When my other two sisters got their periods, my mother announced it to the family at the dinner table with great pride. That was a bit much for me. I was fourteen when mine finally arrived. It was in the morning, and I was on my way to school. I simply changed my underwear, put on a sanitary napkin, and went to school. My mother found out eventually when she asked me about it. She was clearly hurt that I had not voluntarily shared this intimacy with her.

It would be a full year before she would finally agree to buy us tampons. Preserving your virginity until marriage in the Latino culture was sacrosanct, and my mother was a great believer. Unfortunately, that also meant not being able to wear tampons until you were married, lest it tamper with your hymen. The three of us girls rebelled at the dinner table one night. We made a case by pointing out to her that most of our girlfriends at school wore tampons and that it impeded our ability to play sports (especially swimming). When my father spoke up in our support, she relented. Relief! For me, being able to wear tampons was a more momentous occasion than getting my period.

Kica Matos is a lawyer, social justice advocate, and organizer who lives in New Haven, Connecticut.

Nina

I think I was in the seventh grade. I had moved from a private school (class of twelve) to a public school (class of four hundred)—a big change—and had just cut off my braids and gotten my first bra. In class one day, I stood up, and my skirt stuck to me. I twisted around and saw a bloodstain on my tan corduroy skirt. It was only as big as a fifty-cent piece, but it seemed huge to me. Quickly I twisted my skirt around to the front and with my ballpoint pen colored in the spot. That was the official beginning of my career as an artist and the beginning of my staining many, many things: upholstered Louis XIV chairs at the Ritz-Carlton in London and myriad mattresses around the world, not to mention most of my clothes. And even though my period was regular almost to the day each month for about forty years, it always came as a surprise. I was never prepared. And with about nine pregnancies, when the doctor asked, "And when was your last period?" I never ever knew.

Nina Bentley is a visual artist whose work often deals with women's social issues. Her sculpture Corporate Executive Wife's Service Award Bracelet *is part of the permanent collection of the New Britain Museum of American Art.*

Xiao Ling

During the Cultural Revolution in China, toilet paper—the kind that comes in rolls—was tightly rationed. This was really discrimination against having girls. My family—with three girls—used to cope by taking the coarser brown paper towels, which were more readily available, and cutting them up in strips for everyday bathroom use, so as to save the toilet paper for us when we had our periods. Since I was the second oldest, I knew what to expect. But I was still anxious, because I knew the arrival of my period would put a strain on our supply of toilet paper.

At the time, having your period was still something to be kept completely secret. The day my period arrived, my family and I were scheduled to do our manual labor in a local park. We were to do planting, landscaping, and cleaning up. My parents offered to write a note to excuse me from my work, but I insisted that I go. I was so sure that such a note would instantly expose what was happening.

Ma Xiao Ling immigrated to the United States with her family in the aftermath of the Tiananmen Square massacre.

In high school, I told a teacher about the stories my mother and I had heard.

"What if it is something other girls in your class also want to share?" she asked. (Growing up, everyone around me used the words "girls" and "women" exclusively when talking about periods.)

I don't know how to say this, because I think there is a romantic notion I have about a writer on a mission, driven by passion, but I really felt like I was being carried on a current. Someone had to write these stories down. It was the cultural equivalent of sweeping the streets or watering plants. It was just something someone had to do. And I happened to be doing it.

When I think back to high school and asking my classmates to share their stories with me, when these personal histories were all so recent, I feel bashful, even now. I doubt I ever said the words "vagina" or "uterus" or "menstruation" out loud.

Here are some fragments from the few friends I was willing to approach:

T

I was lucky to buy pads. One thing that's different about periods in Kenya is that if you aren't middle or upper class, you don't go to school when you have your period because pads are so expensive. Girls will miss school for a week at a time, and if you miss school for that long, everyone knows why. It makes girls want to go back to school even less at the end of the week. It's so sad because no one does anything to help. Except there is this one guy who crushes plants, and you put it in your underwear to help stop the bleeding. It actually works. I haven't tried it, though.

M

In my family, when you become a woman, you can get your ears pierced. So every year, new girls would show up with their ears pierced at family reunions, and we would all know why: "Oh, there's another one!" I didn't want to get my ears pierced because everyone would know, and I really just didn't see the need. So I waited a year and got them pierced when my sister got hers.

E

The only person at home was my father. And my father is a blusher. He doesn't talk about anything to do with sex at all, so I had to ask him where my mom kept the pads. And he didn't know because she didn't keep pads—she kept tampons.

I asked him to explain to me how tampons worked, but he was so embarrassed that instead he drove me to the pharmacy and we picked up a box of pads. I had basketball practice, and we had to drive up together, as he was my coach. The thirty-five-minute ride was spent in silence. When we finally got there, I blurted out, "It's just my period; it's not that big a deal!"

J

In the bathroom, an elderly woman at the sink said something along the lines of "Hello, dearie, do you know you've got blood on your shorts?"

A pattern emerged. I would talk to one person who would say, "Oh, but you really need to talk to my friend who is a *twin*" or "There is a girl I know who got her period on *September 11*" or "This makes me want to ask my mother or grandmother because I've never heard any of these stories, either."

And so stories started coming my way, in little floods.

Eventually, after hearing enough stories about bleeding, you start to see the world differently. For every moment in history, someone is getting their first period. During the first landing on the moon, during the fall of the Berlin Wall—at that *exact* moment. There is *someone* who has that story.

In other words, it is happening all the time.

I wonder what would happen if we could see history through the lens of blood. Not the violent kind of blood, but this kind of blood. Would we understand governments and policies and war and everything that happens "on high," but down here, where the people are? Could we feel history all the way into our bodies?

Into the World

An assortment of stories I'd gathered with my mother were published as a book. Afterward, I received letters from strangers telling me their memories related to menstruation. I was especially struck by a note from a single father about how lost he'd felt preparing his teenage daughter for her rite of passage, and how relieved he was to have personal stories to share.

Several years later, a theater director in Mexico City adapted that book into a play, and included stories she herself had collected in Mexico. I traveled to see the performance.

I heard the following story performed by three actors wearing all white, on an illuminated plush white stage.

Enrique

I was the oldest of four children, and the only boy. For this reason, I was called "blessed" among women. None of my three sisters ever spoke about periods.

To give you a sense, here is a typical scene from my childhood:

MOM: Set the table for dinner, would you?
MY SISTER: But I have horrible cramps!
ME: Oh no! Did you eat something weird?!
MY SISTER: No, no, this doesn't have to do with food. This is just—
MOM: SHHH! We don't speak of these matters with men!
ME: . . . Okay . . . Do you want me to set the table?

To be fair, at the same time, I also wasn't really paying attention.

Many years later, when I met my wife, we rarely discussed the subject. When my wife was "on her days," I just stepped aside and tried to give her space. The same continued after our first daughter arrived. But when she turned twelve, I received a phone call:

MY DAUGHTER: Dad, could you swing by the pharmacy and buy me some pads? I looked everywhere in the house and couldn't find any.

ME: . . . Me?! Did you already call your mom?

MY DAUGHTER: Yes, she told me she's in a meeting and can't come for a while. Are you busy?

ME: No, no. It's just that . . . Nope. I'm just . . . on my way!

MY DAUGHTER: Get the same brand Mom buys. Kotex. But don't get the purple box. Get the pink one, for medium flow, okay?

I got in the car like an idiot. I *knew* that, for women, bleeding was natural. Intellectually, I understood this. But this was my DAUGHTER. And she was BLEEDING! And okay, I'm afraid of blood! My heart fell to my stomach. Was she in pain? How much blood would she lose? Was there a risk that she could DIE bleeding?! Yes, other women around me had survived, but now that we were talking about my daughter, everything was different!

I got to the drugstore and noticed there were enough kinds of pads to fill entire aisles. That's when I realized that I'd spent my life surrounded by women, but in a tunnel. How? And why had no one told me?! And why did I never ask them any questions?! How could I be FORTY YEARS OLD and so not aware of ANYTHING?!

I started hearing voices, like whispers from my past:

I'm not angry, Enrique!! I'm just "on my days"! Go away!

What are you doing, Enrique?! Don't touch that! That's a women's thing!

Don't worry about them. You're boys. Those are girl problems. GIRL PROBLEMS!

I was furious with myself. I returned to the car with one package from each brand, for each possible heaviness of flow, with options for day and night, slim or wide, and of course one in purple, pink, green, and blue. Plus a pound of cotton just in case none of those worked.

When I got home and saw my wife's face, I knew I'd done something wrong.

"ARE YOU SERIOUS, ENRIQUE?" my wife yelled. "TWO HOURS TO GET PADS? AND WHAT DID YOU BRING HOME? THE WHOLE PHARMACY?"

"Dad! I JUST said the PINK box!!" my daughter added.

And that is how I realized that my "blessing" was just being an idiot.

Theater director Claudia Romero, who penned this story, writes that Enrique is "my brother and a male friend. And the women's voices speak the common phrases in our country." She followed up in Spanish: "La historia de Enrique no es la historia de un hombre, es la historia de muchos hombres, muchas mujeres, muchas familias en mi país, pero sobre todo, es una historia que nace desde otro género: EL TEATRO."*

Claudia Romero is a theater maker. She directs, produces, writes, paints—whatever is needed. She is a theater believer.

---

* Enrique's story isn't one man's story, it's the story of many men, many women, and many families in my country, but above all, it's a story from a different genre: THE THEATER.

When I came home from the play, I started asking odd sorts of questions.

I asked my boyfriend, "Do you have a period story?"

He said, "What do you mean?"

I said, "Do you remember learning about periods? Or . . . did you ever have to support someone through their period? Or . . . do you know your mom's first period story?"

"Not really. No. And, uh, no."

"That is *so* interesting."

"Is it?"

"Yeah, because *not* learning about periods, or maybe even being kind of protected from learning about periods, is actually its own kind of story!"

I came to believe that everyone has a story about menstruation. Even if it doesn't seem like it. And that perhaps *not* having or knowing a story should be closely examined and even considered shocking.

Several years ago, a library in a small city in Brazil was promoting period awareness. The library had selected several books, including mine and a Brazilian children's book called *A Mamãe Sangra*, which translates to "Mommy Bleeds." The book follows the story of a mother educating her infant son about menstruation and the wonderful uterine world from whence he came. I immediately wanted to talk with the author, who I gathered had based the book on her experience.

We corresponded through googled translations ("I am interested in your menstruation book!") and eventually spoke together through the help of her friend. I asked her—it seems like a silly question to me now, but still, I asked in total seriousness—"Where did you get the idea of telling your son about menstruation?"

Claudia

W hy did I tell my son about my period? Because he asked!

I have a personal tradition of collecting my period blood in a jar with extra water in it, which I use to water the plants. One day, my son, Joaquim, saw me holding the jar and asked me, "What is in this jar?" Because he saw blood, he assumed it had something to do with pain.

So I told him. I said, "This blood made you grow. If we take this blood and we water the plants with it, it will make them grow, too."

He was so excited about the idea of sharing this blood with the plants in our garden. I thought, *Wow, maybe this is a new way of educating young people about menstruation.*

Suddenly, I had all these memories about being a teenager and how I had horrible pains around my period. Sometimes the pain was so much I would faint. The boys in my class were awful, too, making fun of me, saying that periods were disgusting and smelled. I remember thinking that I didn't want to be a woman. That it would be easier to be a man.

I felt so emotional, imagining that things could be different. That Joaquim could be the kind of person who could *comfort* girls when they had their period, and say, "It's okay— it's normal." And that he could even look at girls with the kind of awe I saw he had for me, like "Wow, this is something powerful and amazing."

Now, every month when I'm about to start my period, he gets kind of anxious and excited. It's time to water the plants!! He wants to see the fruits on the tree!

In Indigenous traditions in Latin America, blood is sacred.

When I learned this, it was as if . . . a key turned.

For years, I hadn't been able to get pregnant, and a doctor told me I would never have children. My period was this awful reminder of being infertile; it was like a dark symbol to me.

But then I learned that flowing is divine . . . And something changed. My relationship to it changed. I started watering my plants then. And I got pregnant soon after.

Claudia Pacheco runs an alternative medicine clinic in Curitiba, Brazil. She studied Indigenous studies and ancient matriarchal cultures. She is a mother of two.

I found myself sharing Claudia's account with everyone. Its insights felt like a secret I'd been deprived of, due to my Western education and whiteness and lack of relationship with land and place.

Some people already knew the secret, but most did not.

I couldn't let go.

"What kinds of plants do you water in your yard?" I asked Claudia later, by text.

"You can water any kind of plant," she explained. "I like to water the kind that has fruits. In my yard, we water the banana, raspberry, and pitanga trees."

The banana tree that Claudia and
her son water in their yard.

Something in me had changed. Why did I feel comfortable talking about periods now, at age thirty? For years, when I talked about menstruation, I'd felt embarrassed. Then, later, I felt embarrassed about the fact that I still felt embarrassed because I *knew* there was nothing to be embarrassed about! Still, I couldn't help but feel it.

We can take ourselves only so far on our own. Especially in opposition to shame, which is a force outside ourselves. Looking inward is like treating one symptom when the whole body is sick. Thankfully, the collective culture around me changed, bit by bit, and carried me as part of the tide.

This is part of why I believe in books and writing. We are changed by what we read and encounter, in ways we don't even realize, until someday there is a critical mass of people who have been changed in miniscule ways too. And when we recognize one another, it feels possible to speak.

At a small party, I was catching up with a friend. We sat next to each other, tracing little shapes in a pile of salt that had tipped onto the table. While doodling a wave, they asked, "Do you know anything about period negativity?"

"No, what is period negativity?" I said.

"I guess it's something I wish I had heard more about. You know, that it's okay to feel dread around your period, that it's okay to *not* want to celebrate."

"Would you want to write about it?" I asked. "I haven't heard about it, though I think I know what you mean."

Ray

I bled all throughout childhood, in dribs and drabs and little gushes, from my nostrils. In these frequent nosebleeds, I cultivated a certain sense of exceptionalism: through the ability to anticipate the freakish cascade, beginning with a slight, warm trickle behind my pituitary gland; to staunch it stoically with a pinched fist; to bossily correct the boys who tipped their heads back and guzzled their own blood; to leave class in hunched, dramatic exits at random. I could storm out of Hebrew school, trailing cherry-red droplets across the linoleum, and take as long as I liked in the bathroom, making blood mustaches in the mirror.

Yet all good things, in the body as elsewhere, come to an end. In fifth grade, my parents decided that I must stop bleeding from my nose, and I was taken to a tight-skinned ENT in the city, who applied an electrically charged needle to each side of my septum—on different days, so as not to burn a hole all the way through—and cauterized me into bloodlessness.

Then, as I wordlessly grappled with the sad end of this chapter, other kids started to bleed. When a student approached the teacher's desk holding her crotch with both hands and wearing an expression of devastation, I was led to believe it wasn't pee but rather something more sinister, something titillating, both precocious and mortifying at once, that had befallen Bridget. While I looked on from my seat near the boys, dry-nosed and dressed in a gorgeous ribbed tricolor sweater, I realized that Bridget, at the ripe age of ten, was becoming a woman.

By the time I was fourteen, almost all the people who were likely to get a period had gotten it already, had made their special bleeding known, and were taking their own bathroom breaks that lasted as long as they wanted. They were doing other things in there, too, besides filling the feminine-waste boxes, like applying mascara and gossiping and, once, I even smelled, smoking cigarettes. All these transgressions thrilled me with puritanical horror; I didn't need my period to arrive any sooner than it had to.

When it did arrive, hours before an eighth-grade track meet, I embraced menstruation as I did anything I couldn't actively hide or otherwise transfigure: with a kind of ironic distance. ("Sure, I guess dELiA*s has cool clothes for 'girls,'" I'd say with a shrug, since it was beyond the realm of possibility to wear a three-piece wool suit, or make leek tarts on the firestone, or lope along on long, bare feet with shoulders just broad enough to seat my quiver of arrows.) I was now not so different, physically, from those other girls, even as I bore a powerful feeling for Claire Danes in *Romeo + Juliet* that my peers could never be allowed to see. On the other hand, the appearance of my period allowed me to return to a land of exclusive privileges: long bathroom breaks and a mutually beneficial absence from the 4 × 800 relay.

For a decade or so, menstruation struck me as a kind of observational, if inconvenient, joke on my nonreproductive sexual orientation: since I couldn't envision myself ever having sex with someone who could impregnate me, the bleeding felt gratuitous, like my lengthening wisdom teeth or my appendix, beating with unnecessary life. The appearance of a period started to feel wrong—and became upsetting—only when I admitted the distance between my sense of self (suited, loping) and the paradigm of being a woman. But this acknowledgment didn't come with an identity that worked any better. Like the language that flowed continuously among myself and others, spotted with "she's" and my own name, inserting a tampon each month filled me with stinging shame. New humiliations emerged from cold bureaucracies: before medical procedures, regardless of whether there was "any chance that I may be," I was obliged to complete a pregnancy test. I wanted, once again, to be cauterized into bloodlessness.

Yet many bad things, in the body as elsewhere, come to an end. Like watching a cut heal, I wound up with a different identity, different pronouns, binders, and Jim Jarmusch hair, all less painful than what had preceded them. A medley of identifiers—a new name, a flat chest under ribbed sweaters; on special occasions, a jaunty little mustache made of palo santo ash—brought a sense of embodiment made secure not through more definition but through less, through more freedom with associations, new models of coherence.

At a therapy group that introduced me to radical acceptance and multicolored Tootsie Rolls, the mid-meeting recesses were called "bio breaks"—time to accommodate whatever one's biology demanded. I had to use all of my newfound tools to accept the term, but in its bid for both the material and the general, I found something useful. I bleed according to the chromosomally specific but gender-neutral programming that also encoded capillaries close to my skin. And while I could take a hormone to prevent menstruation, the blood that beats through me has long wished to flow out of me, and more and more I'm inclined to let it follow its sanguineous heart.

This New Year's, I found myself nude, abdomen relaxed against the floorboards, listening to the song "Baby Birch," by Joanna Newsom, which spun on a five-tier CD deck. As Joanna cooed, I moved into a plank, and then cobra, and then a series of hectic, nameless positions I would wish upon no one to witness. In that limber hedonism, on the first day of the year, I didn't notice until later the blood smudging my upper thighs, in a pair of Rorschachian blots that remain uninterpreted; I danced until the CD had begun again and the blots were dry. Later, in the bath, I crouched and looked down neutrally at what I thought of, in that moment, as "haunches," as I sluiced the rising water over my legs and the bath grew pink around me. I felt alive, like any animal, and I was glad to be able to hunch and bleed, in the steam, and take as long as I needed.

Ray Lipstein works at The New Yorker.

I wished to share Ray's story with my younger self. Growth is not about "positivity," I wanted to tell little me. Growth is about liberation. And liberation comes from being in touch with yourself. *How do you really feel? And whatever that is, that is okay.*

But how did others feel? And how had their feelings about bleeding and menstruation changed over their lives? And what dimension of the human experience would asking this reveal?

A Small Flood: Stories from Writers & Artists

I asked everyone—artists, mentors, writers, friends:

Do you have a meaningful memory related to menstruation? It could be about a first period, it could be about missing a period, or learning about periods, or any moment that a period marked a transition in your life.

I also asked:

Is there someone else's story about menstruation and growing up and growing older that you'd like to hear? Or wish you had heard?

Whenever I would go out, to the dentist, to the dog park, to a party, I would try to overcome my shyness to ask.

In answer to this second question, many, many people said Judy Blume.

Judy

It's March, a month past my fourteenth birthday, and I still haven't gotten it. My mother reminds me that she was sixteen. How humiliating! Or maybe she was glad because in her day they didn't have sanitary pads and had to use rags. Rags that had to be washed and dried, then used again, and tied on in some way I can't imagine.

One day after school my mother picks me up and says we're going to see her "lady" doctor. The doctor isn't a lady, he's a cold, formal, older man. There's no nurse in the room with us, and my mother is nowhere to be seen. I'm scared out of my mind when without warning, or explanation, he gives me a pelvic exam. No one prepared me for this. I don't want his hands inside me, pushing. It hurts. Never mind that he later assures my mother I'm normal and will get my period. I sob all the way home, furious at my mother for betraying me this way. "Why didn't you tell me what he would do?" I repeat over and over. But my mother has no answer. She seems surprised by my strong reaction.

In April, my bunkmate from summer camp, Stellie, invites me and another camp friend to spend the weekend at her family's lake house. We meet in New York, where Stellie's parents take us to dinner at a swanky restaurant, Danny's Hide-A-Way. After dinner, Stellie's father drives us to the house on the lake. It's late by then, so we get ready for bed. When I pull down my underpants I see a sticky brownish stain. I have no idea what this could be. I've had discharges before but they've been white or yellowish. Nothing like this. Maybe I didn't wipe properly? Ewww . . .

I ball up my underpants and stuff them into the pocket of my suitcase. The next day the three of us go out in the dinghy—a rowboat with a small outboard motor. Stellie pulls the cord, the motor comes to life, and we're off, zipping up and down the lake, the wind whipping our hair as we laugh and sing and have the time of our lives.

That night, the sticky brown stain is back. Again, I ball up my underpants and hide them with the others. You'd think that a fourteen-year-old girl, desperate to get her period, would have a clue what this is. But I don't. It doesn't even cross my mind. Not until Sunday morning when I sit on the toilet, feel something ooze out of me, and look down into the bowl, do I understand. It's unmistakable—it's blood—it's my period! I'm overjoyed. I'm ecstatic. I want to jump and shout and tell the whole world, *I've got it!* But I can't. I can't say anything, because then Stellie and Barbara will know this is my first time and I've been lying since sixth grade, when I pretended I had it just like my other friends.

I nonchalantly ask Stellie for a pad. She doesn't have one but she asks her mother who sweetly asks, "Is this your first time?"

"Oh no," I tell her, "but I didn't expect it because I'm irregular." I know to say this because my mother is irregular, even after having two children, and though I don't know it then, I will be irregular until I'm forty. Then, for the next seventeen years (until I have a hysterectomy) I will be as regular as clock-work. Our irregular cycles don't stop my mother or me from getting pregnant easily when we want to. Lucky us. But at this moment, at the moment of my first period, I have to lie to cover my previous lies. Stellie's mom has no equipment at the house so I stuff my underpants with toilet paper and we drive to town where there is one small convenience store open. They have boxes of pads, but no belts. "Never mind," Stellie's mom says, "I'll give you safety pins when we get back to the house."

It's not the first time I've worn sanitary pads. I've been try-ing them on in secret for two years. I even wore one to school, to prove to my friend, Rozzy, who didn't believe me, that I had my period just like she did. I proved it by letting her feel the bulk of the pad through my clothes. That morning I'd pricked my finger and squeezed some blood onto the pad, in case I had to prove it for real.

When I get home from my weekend with Stellie, I tell my mother my news. I'm not sure she believes me. I think she knows I've been secretly practicing, though she's never said anything. "I got it for real!" I say. (I honestly don't remember my mother's reaction. I like to think she gave me a hug though she wasn't a huggy mom.) I'm embarrassed about those messed up underpants but I throw them into the laundry basket any-way. I have all the equipment in my closet: the pink belt, the box of "Modess . . . because" (same brand my mother uses).

My mother tells my father, who congratulates me. I feel like the luckiest girl alive. It's not so much that I'm a woman, as that I'm normal. And maybe now at last I'll grow breasts.

Years later, I'll write a book about a girl who is as desperate for her period as I was for mine. And when my fourteen-year-old daughter gets her first period, we'll celebrate big time.

Judy Blume is the author of many books, including Are You There God? It's Me, Margaret.

Even more people said:

I want to hear stories about miscarriages.

Stories about period sex.

Stories about not having a "normal period."

Stories about all the shit that happens to your body that no one ever tells you.

Trinidad

A KIND OF RITUAL

I HAD MY FIRST PERIOD WHEN I WAS TEN YEARS OLD.

I WAS PROUD OF MYSELF AT FIRST.

QUICKLY, THAT PRIDE TRANSFORMED INTO SHAME.

WOW!

SHE THINKS SHE'S SPECIAL NOW THAT SHE'S A WOMAN!

AWW, MAN!

CRINGE

I DON'T THINK I'M SPECIAL AT ALL!

TWO YEARS LATER

PUBERTY HIT ME AT FULL SPEED. MY CRAMPS BECAME DEBILITATING. PERIODS BECAME BURDENSOME AND PAINFUL.

GROOAN

I EXPECTED TO FEEL APPREHENSIVE ABOUT MY PERIOD'S INEVITABLE RETURN.

I WAS SURPRISED BY HOW QUICKLY I WELCOMED IT INSTEAD.

AND SO, I LISTENED AS MY SPIRIT TOLD MY BODY WHERE TO PLACE MY HANDS

EXACTLY WHERE IT HURT.

Trinidad Escobar is a cartoonist from Milpitas, California. Her comics and poetry have been featured in literary journals and other publications, including The Nib, *NPR,* The New Yorker, *and more. She is also the author of the forthcoming graphic novel* Of Sea and Venom *and the collection of Queer comics erotica* Arrive In My Hands.

Sarah

No one tells you when you're a little girl that after you give birth, you bleed for a month. Most women learn from their own blood, and most of us don't know how to pass on those lessons, because blood is beyond language, at least polite language.

I wrote this poem after a miscarriage I had over a decade ago:

Miscarriage

When I first said I was bleeding your face changed,
then we went on as before.
Watched comedies on television,
stuffed vegetables into the vegetable drawer.

It wasn't until you saw blood in the toilet,
saw the red unfurl, you let sadness in.
A doctor, you're used to seeing red on white.
You've seen what lives under skin.

Medical sadness waits upon sight;
mine, a mole, needs no light.
Every month women practice for this—
casual loss as a regular thing—

women bleed in private like animals,
men bleed in public like kings.*

*

My miscarriage was on Ash Wednesday, which seemed (I was raised Catholic) somehow appropriate. I walked around Brooklyn seeing ash on the foreheads of strangers and suddenly smelled the metallic odor of blood. I looked around and realized the smell was coming from my body.

For a week, I went to bed and ate Tibetan momos that my daughter's babysitter made (she said I needed iron from some beef) and watched reruns of *30 Rock*. And then I tried to go back to my old life.

*

When I was forty-five, I landed in the ER. I had been bleeding for months, tired all the time, finding myself at one point lying down on the floor in a performing-arts library between the stacks, in utter exhaustion.

Then, while I was on a conference call about an opera, suddenly the blood was pouring out of me in a new, weird, troubling way. I got off the phone and walked to the nearest urgent care. The doctor took my blood pressure, blanched, and sent me straight to the emergency room. They did an ultrasound and found uterine fibroids.

---

* Ruhl, Sarah. "Miscarriage." *44 Poems for You*. Port Townsend, WA: Copper Canyon Press, 2020.

I had surgery, and the heavy bleeding stopped. But the confusion over irregular bleeding remained.

*

When I was forty-six, at the beginning of quarantine, the blood stopped, seemingly all together. The end of my reproductive life was not entirely unwelcome, as I had three healthy children. The hot flashes began, as if on cue. I read that in Sweden and Japan, women don't get hot flashes—why? Did they just not drink as much red wine and coffee as we do in the States? Or was I just drinking way too much red wine and coffee during a global pandemic? Probably. I tried to stop drinking, bought a handheld fan, and took some black cohosh.

And then I started bleeding again. What the fuck?

I bought some pregnancy tests from Walmart and went on with my life.

*

Did my period stop during the quarantine because of global pandemic stress? Transitions are not always neat or final. And the messiness of life's transformations is not often taught in high school health class.

My best friend in high school, Sarah Hinkel, used to faithfully write me notes in study hall. Whenever she had her period, she switched from black ink to red ink. That used to make me cackle. She recently called to tell me the paint company Pantone is now making a red color called Period, but it does not encompass the full range of blood—from the bright-red spot indicating implantation during an early pregnancy to the dark red of a miscarriage.

*

At forty-seven, I stopped bleeding for good. On the early side, like my sister and mother.

The end of a reproductive life is, for some women, the beginning of a *productive* life.

To me, it felt something like a new virginity. I thought:

My brain will be pregnant, not my body, for the rest of this lifetime, at least.

I marked the end of my reproductive life as I celebrated the beginning of my daughter's reproductive life, which coincided exactly.

> *Now I measure time*
> *with different stains, different sheets—*
> *through her blood, not mine.*

*

I think back to that Ash Wednesday:

> *Beginnings and endings are marked with blood. But*
>   *what of middles?*
> *Ash Wednesday, waiting mid-week, mid-body,*
> *full stop in the middle of possibility.**

---

* Fragments from poems published in *Love Poems in Quarantine*. Ruhl, Sarah. *Love Poems in Quarantine*. Port Townsend, WA: Copper Canyon Press, 2022.

*

I'm still in the middle of possibility, trying to thank my body for housing what it chose to house. I also want to thank my body for knowing when to wait and when to let go.

Sarah Ruhl is a playwright, essayist, and poet living in Brooklyn. She is a two-time Pulitzer Prize finalist and recipient of a MacArthur award. Her newest book is Smile: The Story of a Face.

Michelle

Sitting on a toilet in a bathroom stall at Birney Middle School in Southfield, Michigan, I noticed blood in my undies. "Probably hemorrhoids," my mother said when I got home. "They run in the family." She handed me a tube of Preparation H. When the blood kept coming, she reassessed. "Did you hurt yourself on the playground?" I remember her being bewildered. I remember thinking I had cancer. We didn't have the Internet yet, so there was no way to be sure, but I distinctly recall thinking death was near.

Later my mother had her eureka moment and did the parental duty of explaining what caused the blood. "A period," she told me. Okay, a period. I was thirteen, my chest flatter than a piece of matzo. At first, it all seemed to go smoothly. No cramps. Regular maxipads. But over time, it ceased to simply be a period, with a neat final stop. It became more like a series of long em dashes—six super-plus tampons daily for eight days straight. Sometimes I needed two at a time to dam the deluge. Every pair of blue jeans had a dark shadow circling the crotch. In my thirties, I became anemic. I never wore white underwear, and I stained more mattresses than I can count. These periods were five-alarm fires and thrashing thunderstorms—so heavy they often came with gelatinous blood clots that slid down the inner sides of my thighs and occasionally made their way to my ankles.

Gynecologists did all the exams and ultrasounds and scans to see if I had something else brewing below. But no. Nada. Nothing. Take Advil, some advised. Try acupuncture, pelvic yoga. Get on birth control, which would likely lessen the severity of the flow, they said. But honestly, as a lesbian, it all seemed way over-the-top to me. And besides, I read somewhere that the Pill could potentially cause cancer, and the risk, however slight, wasn't worth it to me.

But, as luck would have it, in my forties, I actually got cancer. Not ovarian but breast. *Oh no*, I thought. *Now I'm going to die!* "Not today or tomorrow," doctors reassured me. They'd caught it fairly early, in stage 2, but it had spread to at least one nearby lymph node. So in December 2017, I began a six-month regimen of chemotherapy. Before it all started, my doctors asked if I planned on having kids. I was forty-three and partnered, and the faint desire to bear children had come and gone a while ago. "No," I told them. "But why?" Chemotherapy, I then learned, kills rapidly dividing cancer cells, but it can also damage your ovaries and lead to medical menopause. "Chemopause," they call it. Huh. So much was spinning and whirring around me during those months that I honestly didn't give it much thought. Really, the focus had been on losing my hair, not my period. They also said your period could go away and come back. But for the three years I underwent treatment, mine miraculously moved to Mars.

My partner, Katie, did a little dance. "Does this mean you could wear a white suit at our wedding?" I stashed away my extra-heavy Thinx and stopped buying Tampax in bulk.

This was one of the ridiculous silver linings that came with a possibly dire diagnosis. I lost my hair, sure, but I also lost the feeling—and the very palpable fear—that I was hemorrhaging on a monthly basis. No more tying sweaters around my waist. No more stuffing wads of toilet paper down my pants when I came ill-prepared to work. It was the dawn of a new era.

Seasons changed. Time passed. Pubic hair grew back. I stopped thinking about death every morning when I opened my eyes. Instead fear bubbled up in spurts—when I'd get blood tests or CT scans or step into cancer centers or read about someone whose cancer came back with a vengeance. Or, for example, when I got an abnormal Pap smear at the beginning of a pandemic and had to wait several months for a biopsy. And then, after I did get the biopsy, while I was waiting for the results and naturally assuming the worst, the strangest thing happened.

Sitting on a toilet during lockdown, I noticed blood in my undies and called out to Katie in a panic. "It's from the biopsy," she yelled from the other room. "They told you there'd be some spotting." We bought maxipads and took the Thinx out of hibernation. When the blood kept coming, she reassessed. "Maybe you should call the doctor?" I remember her being bewildered. I remember thinking the cancer had surely come back. I googled "vagina and bleeding and cancer" until I'd diagnosed myself with metastatic everything.

The phone rang. I recognized the number for Memorial Sloan Kettering. I told Katie to come downstairs. She held my hand. "One's thing clear," said the doctor. "It's not a silent landscape down there."

"What does that mean? Ovarian cancer? Endometrial? Uterine? Seriously, I can take it."

"Oh God, no—it's not cancer!" she said. "It's your period."

Michelle Memran is a documentary filmmaker, illustrator, and writer. She divides her time between Brooklyn, New York, and Middletown, Connecticut. She is particularly interested in using creativity as a tool to move through illness. She also plays Ping-Pong.

Daaimah

Not all homes make good shelter. Sometimes a structure under which you stand may provide a barrier from rain, but it also may make you sick. Any number of things can get caught between the drywall and the frame and grow silently until you're inexplicably not well.

If it was fall or spring, I can't remember. I just know I didn't have the protection of a long, thick coat to hide the blood seeping past a supersize tampon, staining the back leg of my bright-purple pants. Standing at the train station after class, I felt a special kind of exhausted. Yes, I had just moved to NYC. Yes, it was my first year at Columbia University for an MFA after not being in school for several years. Yes, I am Black attending an Ivy League institution with Obama newly in his second term (three words: *Before George Floyd*). But that didn't explain why I was too tired to climb the steps at the 125th 1 train station. It wasn't until I got home and took my pants off that I noticed the stain. Deeply embarrassed, I put the pants back on to determine how visible it would have been to other straphangers or, more important, my classmates. I was hoping that the largeness of my ass hid the stain in its shadow. There was a 73 percent chance everybody saw everything and chose to stay silent.

Not all wombs were made for mothering. Sometimes the uterine wall makes space for a tumor or two. Knotty masses that lump onto themselves until it's several large masses that total the weight of a four-month pregnancy.

It took me a while to get to the doctor. Shame is a nasty thing. I kept thinking I wasn't changing my tampons fast enough. I mean, maybe I forgot in between scrambling to add two more pages to a paper and making it to my next class on time. It was only partly a relief to hear the word *fibroids* and know the clothing mishaps were not my fault. Now there were choices to make. Do I have surgery now? In the middle of my first year of graduate school? Do I wait until summer? The severe pain and risk of more mishaps were effective motivators. The surgeon asked casually, "Do you want kids?" He had a look of eternal calmness. Not stern or judgy, which is how I imagined the doctor to appear before I eventually made the appointment. He looked like he might live near 82nd and Central Park West. There is something about being able to see Central Park through your bedroom window every single day that might produce a true sense of well-being. Or so I'd imagined from my desk in Chicago as I'd searched online for places I'd spend my time if I ever scored an opportunity to live in NYC: the Schomburg library, Seneca Village in Central Park, the African Burial Ground near Wall Street.

I got to NYC in the summer, a month before school was to start. My first bucket list visit was Seneca Village, which was located between West 82nd and 89th Streets and Seventh and Eighth Avenues. Today, this area is part of Central Park. Between 1825 and 1856, Seneca Village was Manhattan's first significant community of African American property owners. More African Americans began moving to Seneca Village after slavery in New York state was outlawed in 1827. The African Methodist Episcopal Zion Church also bought several plots on the land. By the 1840s, it had become a multiethnic community of African Americans, Irish and German immigrants, and perhaps a few Native Americans. In 1855, the New York State Census reported approximately 264 individuals lived in the village. It was a stable community, with churches, schools, and cemeteries.

I was excited and full of joy as I approached the site. I imagined I would be filled with pride to stand on a plot of land once owned by Black people during a time before slavery had ended across the country. I entered Central Park at 79th Street and walked north, past the Diana Ross Playground. I stood on Summit Rock and looked east onto a stunning vista. There had been a stable, thriving community of African Americans who lived in harmony with newly arrived Irish Americans right at my feet two hundred years ago. In the distance, I could see the river, then the hills of New Jersey on the other side. There was a cramp in my side. A powerful one. *Not again—I swore I had my period nine days ago.* I sat on a green bench marked with a small metal plaque dedicated TO SILVIA, FOR ALL THE LOVELY MEMORIES OF DANCING IN THE PARK. Now there was pain in my jaw. How tight were the jaws of all the families who'd had to leave this area? Did they get enough money? I stood up quickly. I couldn't share the space with these sentimental benches, knowing what they stood on and for.

The cramps got worse. I didn't know at the time that the fibroids were getting bigger, fast. Maybe where I was standing, the air was so thick with old hurt, it needed a place to shout. And my empty womb was a suitable host.

The doctor put his hand on the desk. He leaned in when he said, "Do you want kids?" I thought of my childhood, beautifully and emotionally complicated, back in Texas. I watched my mother give up so much: her dream of being a concert pianist, her time, and her energy, all in service of raising four kids. I thought of all the parents of Seneca Village, who had worked in good faith to create a good community, only for it to be upended. "Nah," I said calmly, purposely matching his energy. He followed with a description of the procedure: a very quick laparoscopic partial hysterectomy. "Your recovery time will be a maximum of two weeks," he offered as an additional sell.

It occurred to me that perhaps the people of Seneca Village were in such a position that taking the money offered for their land was worth more than the pain of fighting with so little odds of prevailing. I pondered whether my brain is a better womb than my actual uterus. Maybe giving birth to ideas, rather than another human, is more sustainable for this body, at this time.

I put my hands on the desk and leaned close to the doctor, and I told him to "Take it."

Daaimah Mubashshir lives in Manhattan near a park. When she is not writing, her favorite pastime is to sit and people-watch with a friend.

A friend in the theater told me about a show she had directed. Late one night after rehearsal, everyone was going around in a circle talking about their periods. Eventually, the stage manager shared her own story about how not all women, and not even all cis women, bleed. The director offered to introduce us.

Sam

I vividly remember, when I was twelve or thirteen, being hyperaware of periods. I was small, so I was like, "Okay, it might take a little while." And I remember feeling a little jealous. And isolated. And living in anxiety and fear of like, *When is it going to happen?* But the thought never occurred that this *will not* happen.

Flash forward a couple of years to when I was sixteen and I had a serious boyfriend, who was my best friend in that way that is only possible in high school. We were exploring sex and—

Can I be vulgar?

Okay, good. So we're getting down to the point. Penis and vagina meet, and there is nowhere to go. There is an inch of depth, and it's far more painful than it should be.

That mixed with *not* having a period led me to talk with my mom. And then we went to a gynecologist. And that is the *first* place where the medical field failed me. The doctor did *no* exam. And prescribed me birth control.

A couple weeks later, I was still not bleeding. I eventually saw a specialist. He was this old white dude. Not my ideal doctor, but I was like, okay. He did a bunch of exams, and then he said, "You don't have a uterus. You don't have a cervix. You do have ovaries and fallopian tubes. You're going to have to use dilators if you want to have a 'normal' sex life." There was no, "This is what the condition is, here are resources."

Everyone's body is different. There is *no such thing* as normal.

I shared what I was going through only with a few people—my partner and a friend or two—but was not super vocal about it for *years and years.*

I started talking about it when I was twenty-four. I was with someone who didn't cut their fingernails. And there was a tear.

I didn't know this at the time, but my skin is not vaginal skin; it's not as resilient. I was working in this office of stage managers, and I was like, "Can we all do research about what is happening? We all have great brains!"

We found a teaching hospital, and it was at this teaching hospital that I first heard the four letters "MRKH." Having it in my case means an absence of a uterus and a cervix. I have female chromosomes, and I go through hormonal cycles. The gist is I can't have children and I don't bleed every month.

The doctor didn't make a big deal of it. She said, "Of course this is what you have. There are so many people with different kinds of periods. And you will experience what women go through in your own way." I remember her saying, "If you want to do maintenance [using a dilator], you *can.*" It was presented as a choice.

It was like lighting a fire under me. I remember feeling relieved and empowered and wanting to *share.* I remember posting about it online and finding women who were so grateful that I was talking about dilators. I remember feeling so hopeful that I wasn't alone.

I've always felt like a woman. But a big part of me growing up was questioning, "Am I a woman?"

Something that affects the trans community and me, too, that I wish I had heard was: It's okay to not have children. It's okay to be a woman and not have kids. That doesn't make you any less of a woman.

Back in high school, if someone asked me in the bathroom if I had a tampon, I would shut down. Now, if a coworker or a friend asks, I'll say, "No, I don't have a pad, and here's why . . ."

Even in dating, it's one of the first things I bring up with new partners.

Sometimes people are like, "Oh, so I can fuck you without a condom and not worry about you getting pregnant?" The good ones are like, "Okay, let's keep talking, let's talk about how we feel."

It's always terrifying, especially when I'm excited about somebody. But at this point in my life, I'm unapologetic about who I am. And I am *excited* to be that person. And if they don't want to be with that person, then it's not worth my time.

Sam McCann is a freelance stage manager working in live entertainment who loves animals.

I spoke with midwives and nurse-midwives and ob-gyns. They told me of patients who were too embarrassed to come in for appointments on their periods. And how, as nurses, they would have to remind their patients, "There's nothing to be ashamed of. I see this all the time." They told me of young people who asked, plainly, "When our eggs come out, will they crack?" They told me about mothers who didn't know to rest after birth and so bled and bled.

One midwife explained that even *she* encountered subjects around bleeding that felt unspeakable.

Leah

Bleeding is my stock-in-trade. Other people find it gross or embarrassing, but for me, the blood that comes out of someone's vagina is about as exotic as the sweat on your upper lip.

I work in Maternity Triage, which is like an ER for pregnant people. The blood that comes out of women and birthing people is *valuable* to me—it tells me so much about what they are experiencing and what they need from me.

Most people don't know that it's completely normal to have some kind of loss, or what's called "lochia," after giving birth. There's a flow that comes away from the vagina for four to six weeks. It's mostly blood, but it's also tissue from the womb, skin cells, mucus, inflammatory cells, immune cells, all kinds of interesting things. It can taper away and get heavier again. And it can be, I mean, you name every shade of red, pink, or brown, and any consistency. It can be thick, it can be watery, it can be mucusy, it can be stringy. You can have little clots; coin-shaped clots; plum-shaped clots; long, stretchy clots.

When people think they've passed something they shouldn't have passed, we, as midwives, will say, "Is it still on your pad? Can you fish it out of your bin? Can you bring it in so we can look at it?"

I put on my gloves, and I go through it with my fingers. Sometimes I show it to my colleagues, and we'll look at it together. We'll stretch it out. Does it have the solid liverish consistency of the placenta? Or the sheeny, smooth, glossy feel of amnion? That will tell me what it is you've passed. Sometimes we sniff it. The smell is important because different kinds of infection have their own smell. A normal lochia will smell like a normal healthy period, kind of like copper pennies, that metallic but inoffensive smell.

I know how to decipher that knowledge, but more often than not, the birthing person who is producing that blood or clot doesn't know what it means. By being silent about these things, and by being embarrassed, we're actually depriving people of valuable knowledge about their bodies.

The midwives on my unit are very open; we share everything. But I only recently learned that, at some point, every one of us has had an experience of what's called "flooding." Another term for it is *menorrhagia*, bleeding that's heavy enough that it interferes with daily function. It was heavy to the point that one person had to change jobs, because she had a light-colored uniform, and someone else had a hysterectomy. We deal with these hemorrhages all the time—it's part of our daily work— and yet, as a group we'd been private about the fact that we'd been coping with this disaster, month after month, for most of our adult lives, with pretty poor degrees of success.

I think that's really sad, because who knows more about women's bodies than us?

Leah Hazard is a Scotland-based midwife and the author of The Father's Home Birth Handbook, Hard Pushed: A Midwife's Story, *and the forthcoming* Womb: The Inside Story of Where We All Began.

Others said they'd like to tell their stories as a way to unlearn the harmful views they'd been taught.

Kubra

Red Carpet, *by Kubra Khademi. Courtesy of Galerie Eric Mouchet.*

I learned from day one about virginity, but nothing about periods.

I remember how my sister would secretly take care of rags. She would wash them and hang them to dry at night.

When it came, I didn't know it would feel this terrible, this cold, this uncomfortable. And then there was the fear of a stain, of anyone in my family seeing it. I learned that if you pass by a mosque, you don't touch the door, you don't pray, you don't do Ramadan. Because you are dirty.

My mom was married off when she was twelve. She hadn't

gotten her period yet. The day after her wedding, the blood started flowing. A sudden rush—pwoooh!

My dad said, "You are not a virgin," because the blood wasn't "a little bit." For many years, my father said to her, "I was a nice man. You were lucky I kept you."

That little blood that guarantees you were a good woman, a nice woman, that you didn't sleep with anyone—your life depends on it.

Now my mom's period has stopped. In our language, she says, "Now I am a man." There is a sense that now it is "expiration time."

I used to go through depression and pain each month. I learned from Islam that it is good to suffer during this time because we are supposed to "thank God for all the pain he has given me." I felt guilty even thinking about getting painkillers. It's only in the past few years that I've started taking them.

The most terrible thing I learned was not to shower. Where I am from, when you go to the toilet, you use water to clean yourself. Since we are not supposed to bathe during this time, you just sit in it. Only afterward, on the very last day, you are supposed to take a ghusl. A ghusl is a ritual shower, which you also take each time you have sex and when you clean a corpse. Because you are dirty, you cannot pray. And you must "purify" the body.

Kubra Khademi, born in 1989, is originally from Afghanistan and has lived in exile in Paris since 2015. She is a multidisciplinary artist and feminist whose works engage with the identity of women and refugee subjects.

Jennifer

When I was a teen, I associated my periods with shame. The day I first got my period, I called my mother to the bathroom. I was clearly upset, and I asked her if this was my period and whether the blood was supposed to be so red. She looked very uncomfortable and mumbled, "Yes, and yes," and quickly left.

Once, there was a drop of blood on the toilet seat. My father became angry and said he should never have to see that. He said my sisters and I should never want anyone to see our blood, that we should feel ashamed for leaving evidence of our menstruation.

One time, while I was on my period and wearing a pad, my brother had a few friends over. One of his friends pointed at me, saying, "Jenny's on the rag!" and began teasing me. I felt so violated. How did he know? Why was he looking at my crotch area? I hated the word *rag*; it sounded so dirty and ugly.

The biggest cause of anxiety was the lack of pads or tampons in our home. I still remember the feeling of trepidation when I opened the cabinet beneath the bathroom sink upon arrival of my period and the wave of relief to find tampons or pads there, as well as the sinking, anxiety-ridden disappointment whenever there were none.

There were four girls and not a lot of money in our household. When there were no products, it was useless to ask. We were left to our own devices. Wadded-up toilet paper from home and folded paper towels from the bathroom at school were our solution. With these makeshift alternatives, the chance of an accident was tenfold. It left me with a sick, nauseous anxiety every time I got up to change classes at school. The fear and shame of someone seeing my blood was very real, as the only man in my life up until that point, my father, instilled shame in my womanhood.

Struggling through lack of product during my periods was difficult, but far more grievous were the stark poverty of words, the lack of emotional support, and the nullification of feminine strength and identity in my home.

Jennifer Thomas is a mom of four adult daughters and three granddaughters, who are a joy and a pleasure. She is continually rewriting her personal script on womanhood through education and life experience.

Tanaya

This Is What Will Happen to Your Body

In fifth grade, the teachers separated us
by assigned genders: boys and girls.
They told us it's time to learn
what will happen to your bodies.

We watched a VHS tape on a TV
that was rolled into the room on wheels.
PRESS PLAY: *These are the things that make you
a woman, render you female.*

This is what will happen to your body.
The backing track of laughter
of young boys, someday-men
filtered through the porous walls,
scoring the film of our adolescence.

STOP. *This is what will happen to your body.*
The TV is wheeled out into the arena
of your childhood, where make-believe
clouds take shapes that never sing rain.

You are left REWINDING outtakes
from hide-and-seek, where boys
take advantage of your body. Count down from ten—
left with no home base, no "safe,"
just a transparent Ziploc bag filled

with pads, tampons, and deodorant
to capture blood and contain our stench.
This is what will happen to your
body. Changes evident in scent.

In sixth grade, our science teacher, Mrs. Rose,
talked to us about perfume:
Make sure you wear just the right amount.
You don't want people saying, "Ugh, she's in the room."
You want them sighing—

"Hmm, she's in the room"—ready for consumption
as you enter the realm of young adulthood,
body a mannequin on display,
not meant to say a single word.

You are a primal scent, intended to smell
and be smelled. That day my friends and I decided
to guess who would get their period first.
This is what will happen to your body.
We all agreed on an order,
as if any body could be predicted, planned, or

kept like the second hand on a watch.
In school they taught us how to tell time by our bodies
changing, that the arrival of womanhood
was something to be ashamed of.

Outside the classroom, I watched the moon.
The sky taught me the power of being
attuned to her secrets. There is no PLAY, STOP, or
REWIND—
the ceremony of life exists beyond time. The seasons,
our mothers, and their mothers taught us

the sacredness of cycles,
no second hand to unwind. You own your body.
In the moon's phases, I unlearned
Mrs. Rose's bite-size, digestible chalkboard lessons.

Mother Sky showed me
You can never be small or too much
in your unfolding. You are at your most sacred
when you are bleeding, free and untamable,
singing with gratitude. *This is the magic
that happens to your body.*

Tanaya Winder is the author of Words Like Love *and is a winner of the 2010 Orlando Prize in Poetry. Winder is currently working on her third poetry collection. She is Duckwater Shoshone, Pyramid Lake Paiute, and Southern Ute.*

Florence

Getting your period was seen as a symbol of respect and maturity in my all-girls school. It was like being part of a club. Even if we had nothing else in common, at the very least we both bled from our pussy. So if you hadn't started your period yet, it felt like you were being pushed out of and excluded from the sisterhood by Mother Nature herself.

Different sanitary products had a different status. I'm not sure how it was in other schools, but in mine, cool girls used tampons. Being able to "take" a tampon insinuated that you're likely more sexually active, or have "done stuff" with a guy. Although slut-shaming was rampant in school, people knowing that you have sex was also viewed as a sign of maturity, that you were more developed and evolved than everyone else if you had a boyfriend and were having lots of sex. This is why, despite having zero sexual interaction with boys (apart from some hand-stuff on a bench once), I began wearing tampons. Purely for the "cool girl" status. I started off with the mini ones that had no insert mechanism, but those just gave me bloody fingernails. After a few tries at placing larger and larger foreign objects into my body, I upgraded to the mother of all period products: the Tampax Pearl.

Most girls in my class would smuggle their sanitary towels or tampons to the toilet, hiding them under their sleeve so that no one noticed. Not me. I wanted the world to know.

I'd keep a Tampax Pearl stashed in my leopard-print sequin pencil case and pull the zip on it slowly, so that "no one could hear." But the gesture was so intentionally prolonged that it would draw the attention of the girls closest to me. Just what I wanted. I'd purposely rustle the pencils around to "find" my tampon, take a look around the room once I'd found it, and place it under my hand, "hidden" from the teacher. On reflection, it was a little performance entirely for the female gaze. It felt like I was doing *the girl thing*. Like a child who dresses up in her mum's clothes, I was mirroring the behavior of the older girls I looked up to. The ritual of concealing your tampon from the teacher made me feel like a woman. Asking "Can I use the toilet, please?" with my hand in a fist, concealing my luxury blood sponge, I wanted everyone to know it wasn't just a regular bathroom break. The girls next to me knew what I was about to do, and for some reason, I thrived off the validation it gave me.

I also thrived off the bond formed with other girls when they whispered to ask if I had a spare tampon. I loved the assumption that I, Florence Given, must be oh so mature and cool as to have a spare tampon. So I started packing tampons in my bag when I wasn't on my period, just in case the opportunity arose and a girl was in need of my assistance. Perhaps it's no different to asking a stranger for a cigarette in the smoking area of a nightclub. Carrying extras was my excuse for a connection with other girls.

As much as periods had the ability to help me feel connected with other young girls, the shame we were taught to have around them was infectious. We weren't always singing

"Kumbaya" in the girls' loo, passing sanitary towels under the doors. I remember a girl in my school who people used to shame for her period smell. They said she had a "fishy fanny." People would start holding their nose whenever she walked past. If I could go back in time, I would stand up for her, sit with my legs wide open in my navy-blue skirt, and shout, "YEAH, THE SMELL IS COMING FROM ME, ACTUALLY!"

The shame that people who have periods go through, from concealing the tampon to masking the smell to bleeding through your trousers, is another reminder that our bodies are only accepted as pretty ornaments to be looked at. As opposed to functional, divine vessels to be lived in. Periods are literally a part of the circle of life!

A friend of mine used the period blood from her moon cup to feed a plant that hadn't grown in a while. Within a week, it had grown five new leaves. That to me is the coolest, most magical story about periods I've ever heard, and it was very hard not to fall in love with her after she shared this with me.

Women are so fucking amazing and resourceful. The things we're taught to feel shame about by our peers or by systems of power are almost always the source of our power. Because if you were ever to realize the power you hold, it would be dangerous for a lot of people who rely on you being unaware to continue to exploit you. I believe the reason we're made to feel embarrassed about our periods is because it creates this world that cisgender men aren't a part of. It's something they don't understand. So they *had* to poison it. Because if women were ever to form actual connections with one another on a frequency that excluded men, we would be too powerful.

Florence Given is an illustrator, artist, and author of the Sunday Times–*bestselling book* Women Don't Owe You Pretty. *Florence uses her bold slogans and '70s aesthetics to convey her messages and ideas about patriarchy, queerness, self-love, healing, personal growth, and acknowledging the intersections that affect each one of us differently in these areas. Florence is making it her mission to bring women together through her work and encourage us all to realize we are each the love of our own lives.*

There were also many people who said, "Oh, my story is totally normal" or "I don't remember my story." I would say, "That's its own story. People need to know these stories, too." But for some reason, these seemed even harder to write.

I wrote to a scholar in Ireland who I'd met while working on a performance about endings and death. Her research focuses on waste, rot, and life cycles. She wanted to reflect on the question: Where does our menstrual blood go when it's "gone"?

Fiona

I use the sink as a place to think about certain things. Because I spend a decent amount of my time standing there, and there's always more to do.

I used to visit Manu in his apartment, and sometimes when I was at the sink washing his dishes, he would ask me to rinse the filter from his respiratory machine. The gray sponge surprised me the first time I saw it, its porousness, the thin uneven covering of dust. To handle it felt too intimate, a blurring of the boundaries between inner and outer functions. At the same time it felt completely familiar, dealing with dust that is everywhere.

People will leave you alone at the sink; being there indicates being busy. My son will not let me sit at a laptop or tapping on a phone in his company; he doesn't approve of me doing what he can't see. But he'll happily play alongside me while I wash dishes or clean out the drain. At the sink I'm still there with him; he can see what I'm doing and understand it.

There is an advertisement for a period product that shows two hands busy in a sink. Filmed from eye level, the hands rinse and wring a set of period pants. Red liquid flows boldly from them down the drain. It's satisfying to see it. I watched this ad and thought, *I want to do that. I want those hands to be my hands. I want to see the blood.* So I bought the product advertised, and now I find myself rinsing and wringing my own pair at my sink every time I get my period.

Rinsing blood from these pants gives me an aesthetic satisfaction tied to ambient concerns for the environment in a way I know is probably superficial. They offer the constrained level of personal responsibility that works best to sell eco-conscious commodities; the act of ordering momentarily eases the angst of the knowledge of pollution. I'm doing something—I can see it.

There used to be an ad for tampons in which it was suggested their bright-colored wrapping looked so much like candy that no one could possibly believe there was a sanitary product in there. The most important thing about this product, the ad wanted you to know, was that if you bought them, you could hide your period from the people around you.

"Dirt [is] matter out of place," wrote Mary Douglas in her 1966 study *Purity and Danger: An Analysis of Concepts of Pollution and Taboo.* Douglas outlined how the designation of certain things as "dirt" implies a system, an order. In pointing to what dirt is (rejected, inappropriate, best kept out of view), there is an understanding that some other stuff is not-dirt (appropriate, visible, worth maintaining).

For the first years I experienced it, my period was an unwelcome reminder from my interior, a visible demonstration of a potential I didn't want. It manifested in telling spots on light-colored pants, blots on sheets that seeped through onto mattresses, useless scrubbing with rolled-up tissue paper. The unthinkable potential was pregnancy. Getting pregnant was the very worst thing I could imagine. The thought of telling

people was bad enough. I didn't allow thinking of other implications, the birth part, the risk part, the parenting or the baby
part. What caused that dread to seep through me, that notion
that my body was frightening? Some possibilities emerge at
the sink. When I consider shame and the body at that place,
and what has been pushed out of visibility, I think about the
Laundries. The Magdalene Laundries were institutions run
latterly by the Catholic Church from the eighteenth century
until the last one closed in Ireland when I was a teenager in
the late 1990s.

These were residential organizations where women were
sent to live and work after they were considered to have be-
haved impurely or beyond the parameters of what was accepted
behavior. This behavior ranged from flirtation to adultery to
getting pregnant outside of marriage. The symbol was clear:
through doing laundry, scrubbing the sheets of society, keeping busy, and occupying their bodies with a task considered
proper, these women could clean their impurities away. This
system was presented by the Church as a process of salvation
for the women, but it's important to mention the Laundries
were a profit-making enterprise. The Laundries, and the inter-
connected system of church and state that created them, har-
nessed shame around the body, its desires, and its fluidity,
instrumentalizing that shame to conceal women and place
them in servitude. Many women were separated from their
children by this system. A representation could be created
and maintained of Ireland as a place where sex and reproduc-
tion took place only within the clear and visible boundaries
of heterosexual marriage. The traces of this system persist in

many ways; only since a long-fought-for referendum in 2018 have Irish women secured legislation to allow access to abortion.

The historian Carolyn Steedman writes about the persistence of the past and the persistence of dust. The archive, Steedman writes, the collected records of people and their activities, produces dust, the literal stuff of hair, spores, textiles, ash, microparticles, which clings to the researcher and can even make them ill. The persistence of this dust is testimony of the real people who occupied the past—their hands, their hair, their labor; dust manifests the not-going-away-ness of their activities. Dust, Steedman writes, "is about circularity, the impossibility of things disappearing, or going away, or being gone."

At the sink I do the work of washing away with the convenience of running water, drains, and plumbing. These substances rush from me through pipes that join with those of my neighbors, where they mingle with multiple other materials, combine, separate, and become something else but never really go away. It feels satisfying for a while, but there's a persistence to this matter, and that's why I keep coming back to the sink.

Fiona Hallinan is an artist and early researcher, currently working on a doctoral project at LUCA School of Arts KU Leuven. She lives between Cork, Ireland, and Brussels, Belgium.

I wrote to another scholar who studies precolonial Māori rituals, whose dissertation I'd read. I asked if it was possible to share some of her findings.

Te Awa Atua: The Divine River

An essay by Ngahuia Murphy

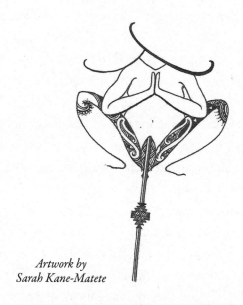

*Artwork by
Sarah Kane-Matete*

*Ko tamawahine te Whare Tapu o te Ira Tangata, te waka
kawe i tētahi whakatipuranga ki tētahi.*

—Dr. Rangimarie Turuki Rose Pere

"Women are the sacred house of humanity, the vehicle that
conveys one generation to another across time." These are the
words of the late elder, wisdom keeper, and sower of ancient
knowledge Dr. Rangimarie Turuki Rose Pere. Her words

reverberate through the cultural fabric of *Te Ao Māori*—the Māori* world. According to the customary language and ritual traditions of Māori, the womb and her monthly cycles are a sacred ceremony that link *wāhine*† to precolonial deities and creation story cycles. The blood is regenerative, assuring the continuation of the people. The flow of the blood—*te awa atua*—was therefore not seen as a women's issue but a family issue.

Traditionally, women retreated to rest and replenish their energies when they bled, with the support of their families. Men procured special food, cooked, and carried the bulk of the domestic chores during this time. They were not excluded from women's menstrual spaces, and Māori histories suggest the men had their own relationships with the blood of life that birthed them into being.

In Māori cosmology, *te awa atua* connects *wāhine* to precolonial deities who comprise the forces of the cosmos. Ancient chants speak to the blood as a symbol of life, whose power is akin to the sun and moon flying west across the sky. Traditional puberty rites celebrated the arrival of the divine river. One of the most sacred puberty rites was returning the blood back to Mother Earth—*Papatūānuku*. This rite reaffirmed the primary relationship between *wāhine* and *Papatūānuku* as one being.

The cultural, social, political, and spiritual fabric of *Te Ao*

---

* Māori: a term for the Indigenous People of Aotearoa, which is known more widely by its colonial settler name, New Zealand.

† Wāhine: a collective noun for women that links back to specific precolonial feminine deities.

Māori continues to be altered and torn through the patriarchal nature of colonization and Christianity. The British colonization of Aotearoa (New Zealand) over the last two hundred years has distorted and suppressed the roles, status, histories, and ritual and political leadership of Māori women. Many Māori families in Aotearoa, through no fault of their own, are unaware of the rich ceremonial traditions that celebrate the blood tides of the womb. There is a massive movement happening in Aotearoa, however, to reactivate *te awa atua* ceremonies and other customary rituals as healing and empowering initiatives. This is happening within the broader context of decolonization and Indigenous autonomy. Ceremonies that have not been performed in over a century, for some families, are being recovered.

Ceremonies that cultivate a deep relationship with *Papatūānuku* are more relevant today, in the context of climate crisis, than ever before. The greatest challenge facing humanity is to restore our "broken relationships to the earth,"[*] which has been redefined as a commodity for exploitation rather than a home. This has led to the ecological crisis humanity now faces. In Aotearoa, many Māori are breathing life back into rituals that remind us that the earth is sacred and the source of our survival. *Te awa atua* rituals are central to the shift in consciousness taking place. Taranaki[†] artist Jo Tito shares her

---

[*] Kimmerer, Robin Wall. *Braiding Sweetgrass: Indigenous Wisdom, Scientific Knowledge, and the Teachings of Plants.* Minneapolis, MN: Milkweed Editions, 2013.

[†] Taranaki: a district on the west coast of the North Island (known traditionally as Te Ika a Māui) of Aotearoa.

personal experience of reactivating the ceremony of returning the blood to *Papatūānuku*:

> *My* waikura* *came on the full moon . . . It was a healing spiritual experience for me, merging with the landscape and listening to the messages that were shared with me. I came home even more determined to honor my sacred blood, to continue to offer my blood in ceremony each month, to honor who I am as a Māori woman, honoring those who have gone before me and those who are to come.*

Jo's comments reflect traditional understandings of the blood as a conduit connecting the generations across time and space. Returning menstrual blood back to the earth is an ancient devotional rite that links the womb of women to the womb of the earth.

Retreating to rest is also being reinstated by some *wāhine*. The following two quotes provide examples of how *te awa atua* is being used as a time for self-care:

> *I give in to rest. I am tired. I have so much I need to reset and nourish for the busy month ahead. I really look forward to* ikura,† *when I can take advantage of more "me"*

---

* Waikura: a traditional term for menstrual blood.

† Ikura: another traditional term for menstrual blood; it links the blood to Māori cosmology.

time. Sometimes I am counting down the days to ikura *so I can run away with my ritual again. —S. Kane-Matete*

I am relishing in my ikura, *big deep breaths, releasing. Today I feel out the other end. Self-healing, self-love, self-assurance—my new everyday practices. —T. Kutia-Tataurangi*

When the blood flows, some Māori are returning to ritualize the divine river as a conduit connecting them directly to pre-colonial deities, ancestors, and descendants. The womb and her ceremonial cycle of renewal are a bastion that represent the survival and continuation of Indigenous peoples and Indigenous spiritualities.

Ngahuia Murphy is a researcher and author who comes from the Indigenous nations Ngāti Manawa, Ngāti Ruapani ki Waikare-moana, Ngāi Tūhoe, and Ngāti Kahungunu. Ngahuia's research specializes in reactivating Indigenous matrilineal ritual teachings.

Sarah Kane-Matete, aka MamaSez, is of Filipino descent and resides in Tūranganui-a-Kiwa, Aotearoa. She is a māmā *to three young children and a full-time artist in the mediums of painting and Indigenous tattoo in both* tā moko *and* tatak. *Sarah's work is inspired and guided by her journey of coming home to self in identity and healing as an Indigenous woman with a strong* mana wāhine kaupapa.

Some people said that their stories, in hindsight, now seemed funny.

Alexis

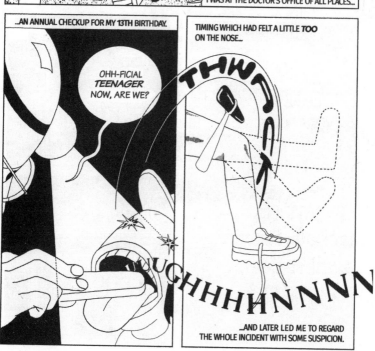

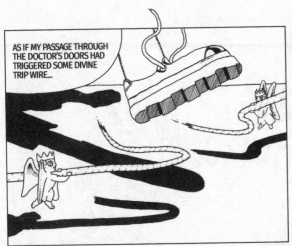

AS IF MY PASSAGE THROUGH THE DOCTOR'S DOORS HAD TRIGGERED SOME DIVINE TRIP WIRE...

...CUEING THE UNIVERSE—PROMPTLY SCANNING, SENSING MY STATUS...

HUMAN: FEMALE

STAGE: ADOLESCENCE

...TO RELAY EXPLICIT INSTRUCTIONS BACK TO THE WALLS OF THE BUILDING:

Do NOT Let That Body Leave Until It Has BLED!

DOCTOR

AND I DID...

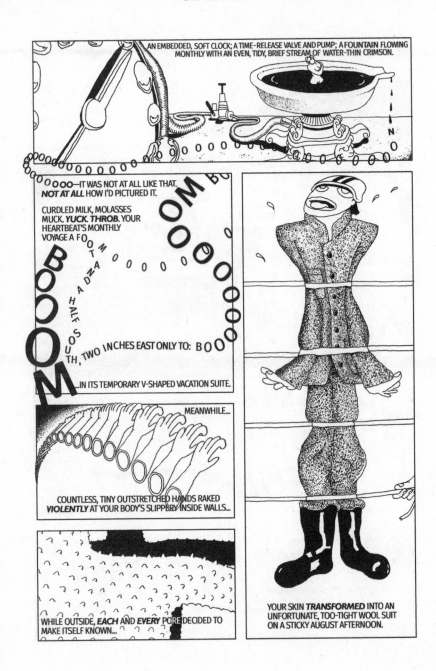

AN EMBEDDED, SOFT CLOCK; A TIME-RELEASE VALVE AND PUMP; A FOUNTAIN FLOWING MONTHLY WITH AN EVEN, TIDY, BRIEF STREAM OF WATER-THIN CRIMSON.

OOOOO—IT WAS NOT AT ALL LIKE THAT. **NOT AT ALL** HOW I'D PICTURED IT.

CURDLED MILK, MOLASSES MUCK. **YUCK. THROB.** YOUR HEARTBEAT'S MONTHLY VOYAGE A FOOT AND A HALF SOUTH, TWO INCHES EAST ONLY TO: BOOM

...IN ITS TEMPORARY V-SHAPED VACATION SUITE.

MEANWHILE...

COUNTLESS, TINY OUTSTRETCHED HANDS RAKED **VIOLENTLY** AT YOUR BODY'S SLIPPERY INSIDE WALLS...

WHILE OUTSIDE, **EACH** AND **EVERY** PORE DECIDED TO MAKE ITSELF KNOWN...

YOUR SKIN **TRANSFORMED** INTO AN UNFORTUNATE, TOO-TIGHT WOOL SUIT ON A STICKY AUGUST AFTERNOON.

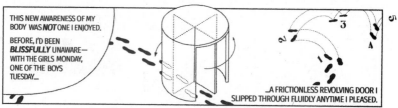

THIS NEW AWARENESS OF MY BODY WAS **NOT** ONE I ENJOYED.

BEFORE, I'D BEEN **BLISSFULLY** UNAWARE— WITH THE GIRLS MONDAY, ONE OF THE BOYS TUESDAY....

...A FRICTIONLESS REVOLVING DOOR I SLIPPED THROUGH FLUIDLY ANYTIME I PLEASED.

BUT **NOW**? WAS **EVERYTHING** ABOUT TO CHANGE?

I WAS HAPPY WITH WHO I WAS AND I DIDN'T WANT **THIS** OF ALL THINGS, TO COME IN AND **MORPH** ME INTO A **STRANGER** WITHOUT MY PERMISSION.

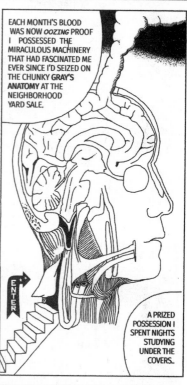

EACH MONTH'S BLOOD WAS NOW *OOZING* PROOF I POSSESSED THE MIRACULOUS MACHINERY THAT HAD FASCINATED ME EVER SINCE I'D SEIZED ON THE CHUNKY **GRAY'S ANATOMY** AT THE NEIGHBORHOOD YARD SALE.

ENTER

A PRIZED POSSESSION I SPENT NIGHTS STUDYING UNDER THE COVERS..

THE THOUGHT **SCARED** ME. AND ON TOP OF THAT—AN UNEXPECTED GUILT HAD SLIPPED, TIPTOEING IN AND ADHERED ITSELF TO MY BACK LIKE AN UNWANTED SHADOW...

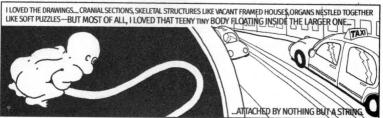

I LOVED THE DRAWINGS.... CRANIAL SECTIONS, SKELETAL STRUCTURES LIKE VACANT FRAMED HOUSES, ORGANS NESTLED TOGETHER LIKE SOFT PUZZLES—BUT MOST OF ALL, I LOVED THAT TEENY TINY BODY FLOATING INSIDE THE LARGER ONE...

TAXI

...ATTACHED BY NOTHING BUT A STRING.

Alexis Sablone is an artist, architect, and professional skate-boarder living in Brooklyn, New York.

Irena

Blood for Dracula

The Western entertainment pipeline was shut down. 1991 brought war and isolation of severe economic and cultural sanctions. Video clubs dried up first. Most new films circulated as shitty camcorder recordings of overseas film projections. Apart from the film itself, the tapes captured shadows of people leaving and returning to their seats. The audio was bad; the lens cap often smacked the camera shell; candy wrappers, soda sucking, and popcorn bags drowned all subtle audio action. The picture dove down to the floor when the camera had to be hidden.

Goran's cousin Sasha worked as an exterminator in America. In his free time, Sasha took his VHS camcorder to Chicago multiplexes and recorded newly released movies. He smuggled the VHS tapes to Belgrade during the holidays as gifts for Goran, who loved horror films. In January 1993, he brought Coppola's *Bram Stoker's Dracula*.

Everyone was invited to Goran's place. The lack of heat and food at the party went unnoticed. We brought blankets and comforters everywhere we went. My light yellow comforter wrapped me into a cocoon. Before the sixth-grade winter break, we were assigned Vuk Stefanović Karadžić's collected ethnographic writings. In a chapter titled "Belief in

Nonexistent Things," the following entry is found on werewolves and vampires. A great primer:

WEREWOLVES AND VAMPIRES

"Werewolf" and "vampire" are two names for the same abomination. Forty days after death, the werewolf rises, driven by Satan. To return from death in this way is to be "vampired" (the word "vampire" is still used as a verb in Serbia, meaning "to become a werewolf"). The werewolf goes around the village strangling people and drinking their blood. To catch a werewolf, take a black horse without blemish to the cemetery and lead the horse over the graves. The horse will not cross the grave of a werewolf. This is where you must dig.

The film quality was great. Sasha recorded an early screening; there were barely any people, and he got the whole screen in. The werewolf was hairy, dark, raw, and hungry, like us. The roars gave us permission to enter other people's covers and clothes. Heavy breathing swelled with music.

When the film ended, a lamp came on, and we surveyed the living room for couples and tears. Everyone cried. We were drying our faces fast. From the left corner came a scream and, after a slight hesitation, an announcement: "Blood for Dracula!" I was sitting on a blanket soaked with blood. I shouted back: "Bleed for Dracula!" Everyone laughed. Not at me. I thought it was a prank. I got up. Cosmic joke. Most of my friends had already gotten their periods. Not during *Bram*

Stoker's Dracula. I stuck half of Goran's toilet paper between my legs and went home.

There were no men or fathers in my family, no prohibition by or preference for men. Menopause, premenopause, and puberty were everyday. The screening brought us continuous entertainment. It also permanently renamed periods to *Blood for Dracula* in our family. *Blood for Dracula* manifested all signs of being visited by a vampire: loss of focus, hypnosis, fatigue, blood loss, immense excess of passions. My grandma wished she still had *Blood for Dracula*, because then she would have fewer hot flashes. During *Blood for Dracula*, my mom had unfulfillable chocolate and fat cravings, mood swings, depression, fatigue, and migraines. The fatigue was immense for me, and the migraines cannot be described in any language; they stop thought. *Blood for Dracula* inflated my sister's breasts at least two sizes. The expansion left white cut marks.

When we went back to school, it followed in the hallways: "Blood for Dracula!" I returned: "Bleed for Dracula!" I used it. With friends, with teachers, in the gym, at lunch, at the post office, in the line for food and gasoline stamps. The war set women back at least a century. Menstruation was no longer mentioned in public, menses was unspeakable, periods ended all conversation, but *Blood for Dracula* everybody understood. It spread:

"Do you have a pad? *Blood for Dracula*."

"Call Todor and his boyfriend. They'll make us laugh during *Blood for Dracula*."

"You okay?"

"No, *Blood for Dracula* came today."

"Uf!"

"My parents left for Germany again. Want to raid their drugs?"

"It's *Blood for Dracula*. Only headphones tonight."

"Hold me up while I throw up. I can't stand straight. *Blood for Dracula*."

"Do you have leftover sugar? I will lick any sugar residues you have. *Sugar for Dracula*."

"Don't go to the protest if you cannot run from the police today. It shouldn't be easy for them just because *Blood for Dracula*."

"Come over, we are here talking and doing hair. *Hair for Dracula*."

"*Blood for Dracula* is late again. Will you come with me?"

"Take only four hundred milligrams of ibuprofen if you don't want holes in your stomach during *Blood for Dracula*."

"Let me know if you need help going down to the bomb shelter. I know you are dizzy during *Bombs for Dracula*."

"It's better to be with women. *Blood for Dracula*."

"Yes! We got some fresh liver from the farm. *Blood for Dracula*."

"Be nice, it's *Blood for Dracula*."

"Stay away from there, too much *Blood for Dracula*. A fucking minefield."

"I cannot reach you . . . I see you in the hole and I cannot follow."

"I am bloated from blood, deeply sunk. In the dark it is dry and cool. If you love me, ask nothing. Just leave some food and cold grapefruit juice by the door. I am in the hay, next to the black horses. The birds are singing and flying over me."

Irena Haiduk's written works and art are bonded by mutual making. To read more, seek out Bon Ton Mais Non, Spells, Seductive Exacting Realism by Marcel Proust 12, *"Studio Feelings," and* All Classifications Will Lose Their Grip.

Sarah

I was not going to be caught off guard. I first read Judy Blume's book *Just as Long as We're Together* when I was eleven. In it, the main character gets her first period on her thirteenth birthday. From then on, I prepared to get my period when I least expected it. Would it be at camp? The first day of sixth grade? On vacation? I braced for the worst, the randomest, the *most* surprising time.

By twelve and three months, I had survived many milestones without disaster striking. Then came the day of my bat mitzvah, the Jewish coming-of-age ceremony I'd spent years studying and preparing for. That morning I woke up nervous at the crack of dawn. Would we get to the synagogue on time? Would I remember the order of the prayers? Was I ready to *become a woman*? I sneaked downstairs and watched the *Friends* Thanksgiving episode with Brad Pitt on VHS to distract myself.

A few hours later, the ceremony went off without a hitch. I led the prayer service; chanted in Hebrew from the Torah; gave a speech about community and divinity; chanted the whole haftorah portion; and chanted sections from the book of Ruth, singing Ruth's famous lines to Naomi: "Wherever you go I will go . . . Your people will be my people and your God my God." It was a lot. When the ceremony concluded, people cheered and threw Starbursts and mini Snickers exuberantly in my direction (to wish me a "sweet" adulthood). I had done it! After years of studying and preparation, I had become a woman.

Victorious and exhausted, I went home to take a nap and change before the party that evening. And that's when I discovered that at some point between Brad Pitt and the book of Ruth, I had become a woman all over my underwear. And man, was I caught off guard. What kind of a sick joke was this?! There's a Yiddish saying: "Man plans; God laughs." The Judy Blume version is "Girl plans; God gives first period on bat mitzvah."

I went into my mom's room and found her blessedly alone. "I think I just got my period," I said glumly. She looked at me, dumbfounded, but recovered quickly. "Mazel tov!" she said, and handed me a pad. My biggest fear was that she'd go down into the living room filled with my entire extended family and announce the news: today Sarah became a woman, twice! (To her credit, she didn't.)

When I came downstairs, I awkwardly told a couple female friends, both a few years older than me. They squealed and hugged me. But I felt strange. Uncomfortable. Jet-lagged, like everything had changed but I was still stuck in the earlier time zone. The joyful transition into womanhood—the ceremony, the candy thrown at my head, the party with a DJ—had been amended by reality. Blood at inconvenient times. Uncomfortable conversations. Adulthood seemed like kind of a burden, but there was no going back. So like the Jewish women before me—from Ruth and Naomi to my mother and my friends—I prepared to bleed for the next forty years at inconvenient times. With this new weight upon my shoulders, I stuck the pad to my underwear and went to my bat mitzvah party, where I danced until ten to Christina Aguilera.

Sarah Rosen is a writer and filmmaker.

Tamora

Unlike a lot of girls at that time, I knew quite a bit about what to expect. My mother, who had studied nursing for two years, had been careful to explain the Facts of Life in a way I could understand from the time I was very young. Around about fifth grade, I discovered I could put off bedtime if I asked her to explain to me about the uterus and the ovaries again. (She drew pictures, which was time-consuming for her and more stay-up time for me.) I was a problem child for the poor teacher who was given the job of (highly controversial and new) sex education for girls, because I would show off my learning and use the scientific terms when I asked questions. (Okay, I admit it, I was a geek as a kid.)

I spent fifth and most of sixth grade in a state of high excitement, waiting and hoping for that first period, the sign that I was a woman at last. I knew it would be soon, because when I bounced and watched myself in the mirror, I began to see jiggling, which was my mother's bottom-line requirement for a first bra. Until the boys in my sixth-grade class noted it, I hadn't realized I was getting hair under my arms—another milestone. So I waited, even though it seemed like I waited *forever.* I can still see the time and place where I got that first hint. In the hall outside our sixth-grade classroom, as I was walking down the stairs, I felt some kind of slipperiness between the cheeks of my rear. It never occurred to me to look until I was home. My parents were out, we had a babysitter, and I startled her immensely by joyfully screaming, "I've got my period! I've got my period!" She celebrated with me, having reached that longed-for state two years before me. The first thing I did was find the pads and the little belt (in those days, you either hung a pad off a little belt inside your underwear or you pinned it to your underwear—no stick-on napkins then), assemble them as my mother had shown me, and put my first napkin on. When my parents came home, I got hugs and congratulations.

By the next day, I was introduced to the downside of having a period: my first, very mild case of cramps as my parents wondered if I should go to a roller-skating party. In later months, I would learn about worse cramps, lower back pain, and the fact that you can't wear a napkin to a swimming party, which included a painful first introduction to a tampon. But I have never forgotten those first few hours, the slippery feeling that led to triumph, that feeling that I'd passed the last test of womanhood and could conquer the world.

Tamora Pierce is the #1 New York Times *bestselling author of over eighteen novels set in the fantasy realm of Tortall. Her writing has pushed the boundaries of fantasy and young adult novels to introduce readers to a rich world populated by strong, believable heroines. In 2013, she won the Margaret A. Edwards Award for her "significant and lasting contribution to young adult literature." Pierce lives in Syracuse, New York, and spends her free time herding feral cats.*

Hannah

BY THE TIME I TURNED 15, I THOUGHT OF MYSELF AS A PRO AT HANDLING MY PERIOD...

BEST PAD DURING DAYTIME ✔

THIN

WINGS ✔

SUPER LOOOOOONG PAD FOR OVERNIGHT ✔

2 Year Period Veteran!

STAIN-FREE ✔

...UNTIL THE FIRST TIME MY
PERIOD FELL DURING A
<u>MODEL</u> <u>UNITED</u> <u>NATIONS</u> WEEKEND.

MODEL UN WAS THE MOST POPULAR CLUB
AT MY HIGH SCHOOL. SURE, LEARNING
ABOUT FOREIGN AFFAIRS AND PUBLIC
SPEAKING WAS GREAT, BUT I LOVED IT
FOR <u>OTHER</u> <u>REASONS</u>, TOO...

BOYS IN BUSINESS SUITS!

WEEKEND TRIPS TO CITIES & COLLEGE TOWNS!

OVERNIGHT HOTEL STAYS WITH FRIENDS!

AS A HIGH SCHOOL STUDENT, I LOVED DRESSING IN BUSINESS ATTIRE FOR MODEL UN,

SO POLISHED

SO CHIC

SO GROWN-UP

BUT I WAS ALSO SELF-CONSCIOUS SOMETIMES ABOUT THE SILLIEST THINGS.

♪ my pantyline shows, got a run in my hose... ♫

FOR SOME REASON, I WAS DRAWN TO CLINGY PENCIL SKIRTS (THANK YOU, ALLY McBEAL*?!). TO AVOID THE DREADED Visible Panty Line,

I THOUGHT T<u>H</u>ONG <u>UNDERWEAR</u> WAS THE ANSWER.

* VERY POPULAR '90S SHOW ABOUT SEXY LAWYERS IN SEXY SUITS

** I WAS IN HIGH SCHOOL WHEN SISQÓ'S "THONG SONG" WAS AT THE HEIGHT OF ITS POPULARITY.

baybeeee that thong th-thong thong thong

BUT HOW THE HECK WAS I GOING TO HANDLE WEARING A PENCIL SKIRT AND ITS NECESSARY, ACCOMPANYING THONG AT THE HEIGHT OF MY PERIOD?

WEAR REGULAR "GRANNY PANTIES" WITH A PAD AND DEFINITELY GET VPL?

PLUS BULKY PAD SHOWING THROUGH

WEAR A REGULAR PAD WITH A THONG?!

MY BIG SISTER WAS 3 YEARS OLDER THAN ME, AND I KNEW SHE USED TAMPONS.

Playtex

MY PARENTS WERE SOCIALLY CONSERVATIVE KOREAN AMERICANS, AND THEY NEVER TALKED TO ME ABOUT BODIES, PUBERTY, OR SEXUALITY. WHEN IT CAME TO TALKING TO MY PARENTS, ANYTHING RELATED TO MY VAGINA FELT LIKE IT WAS OFF-LIMITS.

THE NIGHT BEFORE THE MODEL UN TRIP, I DIDN'T KNOW WHAT TO DO ABOUT MY PERIOD, SO I JUST THREW EVERY OPTION INTO MY OVERNIGHT BAG.

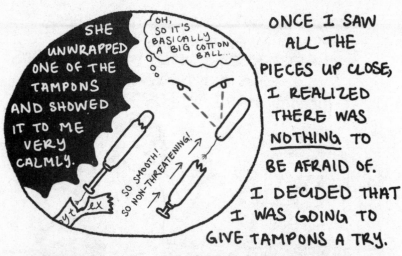

ONCE I SAW ALL THE PIECES UP CLOSE, I REALIZED THERE WAS NOTHING TO BE AFRAID OF. I DECIDED THAT I WAS GOING TO GIVE TAMPONS A TRY.

I HEADED INTO THE BATHROOM OF OUR HOTEL ROOM WHILE MY FRIENDS WAITED OUTSIDE.

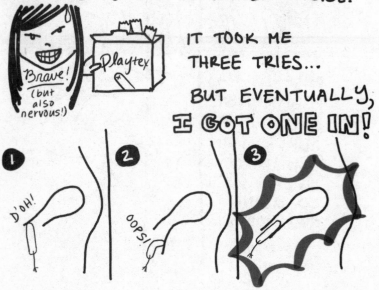

Hannah Bae is a Korean American writer, journalist, and illustrator. She is the 2020 nonfiction winner of the Rona Jaffe Foundation Writers' Award, and she is working on a memoir about family estrangement and mental illness.

For one artist, her period had even sparked her relationship to comedy as a way to cope with what we can't control in this world.

C.C.

THE CIRCUS
TENT IS A
GOOD METAPHOR
FOR THE
WHOLE SHOW
GOING ON
INSIDE

I took a break from bleeding for five years. The fifth year fell during a pandemic, and I feared that if society collapsed, my body would eventually fuse with the hormone device in my uterus like a tree consuming a chain-link fence. I used similar logic for my low-maintenance hairstyle. It would be easier to survive without needing a professional's help.

When I got my first period after the IUD removal and woke up to fresh stains on my new white sheets, I felt like an emotionally underprepared thirty-five-year-old teenager. As I dabbed bleach on the spots, I had flashbacks of my younger days when I bled on a borrowed swimsuit, a bike seat, a brand-new mattress, and a chair in a crowded auditorium during a two-hour lecture.

My collected memories of multiple period accidents have transformed into a mild but persistent fear: no accident is ever the last. I habitually manage fear with nervous laughter to make any situation feel less horrible. I even laugh in my sleep when having a nightmare. If I don't take things too seriously, then maybe the impact of those things won't be too serious.

Just as laughter helped me win friends as the new kid at a succession of public schools, humor later helped me fit in on the Internet—an escape from the limits of my reality the moment I typed *I'm bored* on the school library computer and found Myspace and AIM. Suddenly I was typing with someone else somewhere else.

Each joke I made about my period became less guarded than the last and brought me closer to serious critical thought.

Thinking about my period meant I was also always thinking about cultural settings, the environment, power structures, states of mind and mood, capitalism, and gender politics as much as the basic biology of cyclical bleeding and breeding.

In my twenties, I created art texts of self-aware observations about my period and life. They inadvertently served as an intimate education between me and my own body. Keeping an unserious record of my mysterious sensitivities led me to see patterns, like how I seem to have an easier time dealing with my body when I am alone, instead of pretending I am "normal" while my internal reality slowly bleeds through to the external reality of a very long work meeting.

I still don't know everything, like how not to have an accident on my bed linens. I will always be the new student trying to fit in. With each period, I have a little laugh and I get a little wiser about the whole show going on inside.

I TRIED TO PUSH IT ALL OUT
BUT IT DIDNT WORK

I HAVE AN OUT OF BODY EXPERIENCE
ONCE A MONTH

C.C. is an artist using text, image, performance, and sound to write poetry.

A friend who I'd collaborated with on a project about feminist utopias encouraged me to write to several incarcerated writers she works with.

Elena

Elena House-Hay is an incarcerated individual, artist, and writer who has found freedom in art and purpose in finally speaking up.

Zhi Kai

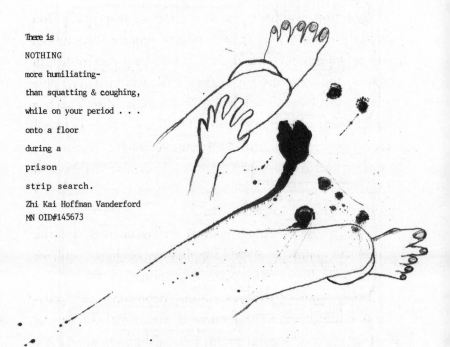

There is
NOTHING
more humiliating-
than squatting & coughing,
while on your period . . .
onto a floor
during a
prison
strip search.
Zhi Kai Hoffman Vanderford
MN OID#145673

I came to prison in 1987. I was nineteen years old.

Periods aren't fun anywhere, but when I first got to prison, you had to buy feminine hygiene supplies and only pads were available at the canteen (the prison-run store). We were paid eight cents an hour at our prison jobs, but ten pads cost three dollars. The prison provided emergency pads only if you had not had the opportunity to shop at the canteen that week.

Pads always made me feel like I was wearing a diaper, and while I was not thrilled about penetrative devices, they seemed more hygienic and less like an advertisement that I was having a period.

In prison, we made our own tampons from pads: You carefully open the pad at one end and remove the stuffing, only keeping about half. You roll it into your custom-length tampon and then insert it back into the pad liner. The glue side gets rolled onto itself, and the top is knotted for a tea bag string. There are no applicators. These homemade tampons were considered contraband, so you didn't make too many at a time. If guards found them, they would confiscate them and threaten to write a report that you were destroying or misusing property. They never did, though.

I think I was twenty-five when the law changed and the prison had to provide us with supplies free of charge. Still, we had to ask male guards for a pad or tampon.

Being a trans male, it is so dismal, depressing, embarrassing, and mortifying to have a period. Menstruation for me is another form of imprisonment, like my body betraying my very essence. As a teen, it was said to me that it was a sign that I was a woman. It meant I could have children—which I have many adopted but none biological—and that it was natural. But natural FOR WHO!? I didn't ask to be a woman.

Now Minnesota's women's prison has bins of small and large tampons or pads available, without you needing to beg officers. I'm fifty-three and haven't had a period in a long time, but it almost makes me wish I had a cycle for the freedom of taking what I need when I need it.

Zhi Kai Hoffman Vanderford is a driven activist, eloquent poet, and motivated artist for human rights. He has been incarcerated for fifty-three years in the wrong body and for thirty-four years in prison. He is working on his master's degree with future hopes of helping LGBTQI youth navigate their lives.

Kwaneta

In prison, we're strip-searched often. Before we leave our cell. Before and after work. Each time we must remove our pad or tampon. We're assigned one pack of pads and five regular-size tampons monthly. If you're one of the heavy bleeders, women who have fibroids or are premenopausal, the state will not provide you any extra items. You must purchase them, which means family must send you money, or you befriend an older lady who no longer needs them and you trade her soaps, medications, etc. for pads. We aren't paid to work in Texas. And nothing is free in prison.

Many of us work in the fields, tending crops under the watch of armed, mostly male, guards on horseback. At the end of our workday, sixty people crowd into a space meant for thirty. The female guards stand in the front as we strip. We must stand there nude until it's our turn. We must remove our tampons and pads while we wait in line. It's common to see trails of blood running down a leg or to step in blood as we move closer to the front. They used to have a box of pads for after we were searched—squat, bend over at the waist, spread our buttocks, lift our feet, turn around, raise our stomachs and breasts, tip our noses skyward. Due to budget cuts, we must bring our own assigned pads or tampons. Sometimes it's not enough, and you use toilet paper in your panties when dressing. It's bad enough to do such a thing in front of women. But the male guards all put on their sunglasses and stare at a circular mirror posted outside the stripping area, which they call a bullpen.

We get only three pairs of panties every four months. If you have family, you can purchase more, but we are allowed to have only seven pairs of panties total. During cell inspections, I've seen male and female guards take someone's period-stained panties out of the cell, hanging them off a pen, to mock them. I've had guards open every single pad and tampon to check for contraband. Now the tampons are contaminated. There's no need to open a sealed package, but they do. I'm just so thankful I can afford the eleven-dollar box of tampons to replace them.

Our prison clothes are all white (except for socks, which are gray). With wearing all that white and in an all-female prison, accidents happen. Once I heard a guard belittle a lady, telling her, "You just nasty. You get cramps—you knew it was coming. You just trying to get out of working. I'mma make you stay and work." He called her a bull's-eye [because of the] big red spot on her pants.

The solution for many women who are indigent is to get the birth control shot, thus eliminating their periods and the risk of embarrassment.

Kwaneta Harris is an incarcerated mother of three, living in solitary confinement with a wish to hug her children.

A Brief Interlude on Menstrual Justice

(Or, What Is Menstrual Justice?)

Several years ago, an electronic musician ran the London Marathon while free-bleeding. By the finish line, menstrual blood had seeped through her athletic wear. Photos of her, with her arms raised and her clothing stained, made headlines.

I keep trying to reframe for myself what is shocking about this story. What is shocking is not that someone publicly bled, but rather, that it is *considered* shocking. That it makes *news* when someone chooses to avoid chafing and pain for twenty-six miles instead of just grinning and bearing it.

A Conversation
with Madame Gandhi

RACHEL

The story of you running the marathon while free-bleeding is so inspiring to me. I want to know what your relationship to periods was like before that. Like, how do you *get* to a place where you decide to run a marathon and publicly bleed?

MADAME GANDHI

I was getting ready to move from LA to go to Harvard Business School, and I was also getting ready to drum for M.I.A. on tour.

One morning, I was in a Starbucks and my period cramps were so bad, I fainted. Never in my life had I fainted because of my period. But I hadn't eaten anything that morning, and possibly nothing the night before.

I woke up in the hospital, and I remember feeling like my period had *revolted* against me. When in fact, it revolted against me because I hadn't nourished her the way I needed.

I never wanted to feel that way ever again in my life. So around my cycles going forward, I made sure: I'm eating, I'm sleeping, and I'm drinking water.

For the next few years, I was honestly afraid of my period.

When I got to the start line of the London Marathon, I realized it was going to be the first day of my period. I was caught off guard. Because usually, when I had it, I wouldn't work out. Sometimes I wouldn't even go to class. I mean, I really didn't want to do anything assertive or overdo it.

I thought, *What am I going to* do*?! Today is marathon day!*

I started evaluating my options:

I don't have a pad. Chafing causes a lot of discomfort. I don't have a menstrual cup on me. I don't have a tampon—I didn't want to have a half-in, half-out situation! Plus, there's no privacy on a marathon course. Moreover, I was afraid because of my experience in the hospital. So I decided I would rather bleed freely than mess with my body in any way—and just run.

Bleeding from anywhere is a punk rock move, if you ask me—especially for twenty-six miles! And yet, as I ran, I thought, *I am privileged to be able to choose what's best for me and my body; millions of women, girls, trans folks, and people who bleed are not.*

Stigma is one of the most effective forms of oppression. It's so effective because none of us question it: We hide away in silence. We can't educate one another. You can't celebrate the wins or bond over the pain.

When I crossed the finish line, it was a monumental shift. Not only had I felt strong during my period, but I had run a marathon. And I didn't feel any shame free-bleeding because I was like, "How can you shame someone running a marathon bleeding from *anywhere*?!"

RACHEL

What does that shift feel like?

MADAME GANDHI

It's like stepping into your own power.

It's like big boss energy.

Or actually, it's like telling the truth.

I just told the truth on that day at the marathon: I don't have a tampon and I just want to run.

But I should say that the most transformative part of the experience was actually writing about it.

I never ran with the intention of creating a viral moment. I ran with the intention of crossing the finish line by any means necessary.

It was a private experience—people couldn't even really see that I was free-bleeding—until I wrote about it and shared photos.

I wrote about the stigma, too. About how we have a disproportionate luxury tax on tampons, and the fact that homeless women and incarcerated women and women in low-income communities don't have access to the products they need. I wrote about how we don't talk about the trans community when we talk about periods and the fact that we are still using carcinogenic products in the most sensitive parts of our bodies.

And that's what went viral. The article.

RACHEL

Is there anything in recent years you've learned that you'd want to add to that list?

MADAME GANDHI

One thing I want to change is the use of the term "feminine hygiene products." It should be "menstrual care products."

RACHEL

The patriarchy is everywhere! It's in all our languages! It's under every rock! *Thank you* for bringing all these issues to public attention.

Madame Gandhi is an LA-based artist and activist known for her uplifting, percussive electronic music and positive message about gender liberation and personal power. She has been listed as a Forbes 30 Under 30 in Music, and her 2020 TED Talk about conscious music consumption has been viewed over a million times.

For the first time in my life, during the pandemic, I saw flyers out in public asking for donations of menstrual care products.

A group of high school students in the Midwest were particularly active in distributing free period kits to those in need. I wrote to their collective and asked if I could speak with them on a day they weren't all too busy with school.

A Conversation with Amira & Amy & Anika & Maggie of Bleed Shamelessly

RACHEL

Thank you all for taking time on a school night! Maybe we should start by talking about how you got involved with menstrual equity and your organization, Bleed Shamelessly?

MAGGIE

The way it started was that I was a part of what was then called the Women's Club at our high school, which is now the Gender Equity Association. It started small, as a two-person initiative to destigmatize menstruation. We've since grown into an organization that wants to speak to *all* issues relating to menstruation, menstrual equity, and reproductive justice.

AMIRA

I first heard about Bleed Shamelessly because Maggie mentioned offhand, "Oh yeah, by the way, I kind of started a nonprofit and we're working to end period poverty." And I was just like, "I'm sorry, you did what? You're like one year older than me and you have all of this organized!"

AMY

I think the first volunteering thing I really did was help package menstrual care product kits.*

MAGGIE

One of our first big events was to host the National Period Rally for Wisconsin to eliminate the luxury tax on period products.

RACHEL

I'm realizing we're using some terms that might be new to people. Would you all be able to explain, to someone unfamiliar with menstrual equity, why organizations like Bleed Shamelessly need to exist?

AMIRA

So organizations like Bleed Shamelessly exist because many menstruating people do not have access to safe and affordable means to care for their body. Products such as pads, tampons, and menstrual cups are simply too expensive. In many states, period products are taxed as luxury items. But they are also expensive because we live in a capitalist society where prices are incredibly high, whereas wages are incredibly low.

---

* In response to the COVID-19 pandemic, Bleed Shamelessly organized volunteers to pack over five thousand kits and ninety thousand individual period products for their local county.

Menstruating people face a barrier of not being able to access the same things as non-menstruating people. And they're supposed to do this behind closed doors and effectively suffer in silence.

For example, many folks need a certain type of period product. It's kind of like if you have a fatal allergy. Some individuals can only use products that don't have certain types of chemicals. Or if someone with a disability can't grasp a tampon to pull it out, it could get stuck inside. And that is incredibly dangerous. So a lot of folks are left with unsafe means.

Many folks would just free-bleed, which is when you don't wear a pad, you don't wear a tampon—you just let it come out and it goes in your pants. But a lot of employers, schools, and places of business will kick you out if you are visibly bleeding.

So a lot of menstruating people are left with the choice to buy products they may not be able to afford, or they cannot go on with their life. This can decrease someone's pay. Someone could be fired if they miss a certain number of days. Or someone may miss school and fall behind. And then that is problematic in a world that requires basically perfect attendance.

Menstrual equity impacts historically marginalized communities differently. For instance, BIPOC, low-income, immigrant, trans, nonbinary, and gender-expansive communities are less likely to have the means to afford period products because of systemic barriers in our current economic system.

There is also no widespread awareness that men menstruate, nonbinary people menstruate, two-spirit people menstruate, and that people of any and all genders or no gender at all can and do menstruate. If you are a trans person who cannot go into the women's restroom because you don't appear to be a woman, you might get thrown out or arrested because, when a masculine-presenting person enters the women's restroom, the assumption is that they are a threat. But if you go to the men's restroom, there are simply no period products. There are all these locked doors that present themselves.

ANIKA

One thing I want to add is the way that menstrual equity translates to our local community, which is in school. In our school district, they don't provide period products in men's or gender-neutral restrooms.

RACHEL

Thank you! To take a step back, how did you all become so comfortable talking about periods?

ANIKA

Throughout middle school, it was something I felt really uncomfortable talking about. I think that's because of how we're socialized. It's the norm in culture that we don't talk about menstruation.

But when I got to high school, I grew more aware of reproductive justice and our society's emphasis on controlling our bodies, and I started unlearning all this inherent misogyny and sexism.

AMIRA

Similar to Anika, my middle school had created an environment that was really stigmatizing. It was not talked about among teachers and the staff members. I would always put my tampon up my sleeve.

Also, there weren't period products in *any* bathrooms. The school didn't even buy period products for the *nurses*. It just wasn't on the agenda. Overlooking what so many students need, especially because those products are expensive and a lot of students don't have them at home . . . it was just jaw-dropping.

I would say that things changed when I had a kind of "second first period," after my transition to being nonbinary. I was unsure of how I would react. I was starting to get dysphoria around different parts of my body. I was bracing myself mentally. Being in spaces where trans menstruation is openly talked about really helped me get to the point where I could be like, *Yeah, I menstruate. I'm trans, and I'm okay with it. So you better be okay with it. And if you're not okay with it, that's your problem.* I feel more in touch with myself after that experience.

AMY

My family is pretty reserved. So my mom never talked to me about this. I watched these YouTube channels that teach you life hacks for what to do when you get your period. Like, "If you have an Elmer's glue bottle, you can hide your tampon there!" My friends and I had all these code words we would use. I would say, "Red Pen."

I knew there was stigma, but I never realized it was a problem. I kind of accepted it, especially because I was prepared from all the life hacks! Until Bleed Shamelessly's rally, I never actually questioned the stigma. And I was like, "Wait, it's such a normal thing . . ."

MAGGIE

I'm going to cry, Amy!!!

RACHEL

What kind of futures do you *hope* for? What are you and your friends involved in menstrual justice—not just working toward practically, but really dreaming of?

MAGGIE

I would like to live in a world where no one is inhibited by any sort of bodily function, in the sense that society no longer tells certain people with certain bodies that they are wrong for having those bodies or that those bodies are inherently disposable. And those bodies range from so many different things, from menstruating bodies to Black and brown and Asian bodies.

A common response we get when we say, "Menstrual products should be free" is, "Oh, well, by that logic, food should be free." And our response is always, "Yeah, it should be!" Necessities, things that people need to live, survive, and thrive— food, shelter, health care, education—should be free! And everyone should have access to them.

ANIKA

Sounds pretty great. I'd like a world in which businesses, the government, and schools supply menstrual products to everyone who needs them. In that world, we'd shift the conversation to be more inclusive of all menstruating folks.

And also just talking about menstruation more! Like talking about menstruation in your family, because it's kind of like starting at those root levels. If you have a family that doesn't talk about menstruation, that starts building up the stigma in your brain.

AMIRA

I really resonated with that, Anika, and how you were talking about the importance of inclusive language. The mainstream menstrual movement is very white. It's very cis. It's very straight. This compounds the erasure of trans, BIPOC, disabled, neurodiverse, low-income, immigrant, all other historically marginalized identities. Menstrual equity isn't just for some people. It won't be achieved completely if only the straight, white, skinny women can access it. We have to keep pushing until everyone has access. And that does include lots of other systemic changes, meaning living in a society that is invested in care as opposed to punishment.

We also need to be able to support one another publicly when it comes to menstruation. So people can call their employers and say, "Look, I am having absolutely awful cramps today, and I just wouldn't be able to do my best work. Can I have a sick day?" People don't have to share about their period necessarily if they don't want to. But I'd like to see a world where there aren't cultural barriers.

MAGGIE

What you just said made me think of how someone for a Bleed Shamelessly project texted me and was like, "I'm having really bad cramps right now. Is it all right if I don't come to this meeting?" And I was like, can you imagine if I said no? Even organizing culture can be exploitative, so that is all super important to think about.

Amira Pierotti (they/them) is a youth activist for transgender and gender-expansive rights, menstrual equity, and sexual assault survivor rights. They are a Lead Organizer with Bleed Shamelessly, a student facilitator of GameChangers, a student representative on the Rape Crisis Center board of directors, and an advocate with a statewide coalition to end transphobia in Wisconsin.

Amy Yao (she/they) is a teen activist who's involved with her school's Gender Equity Alliance. Amy is passionate about environmental, racial, and reproductive justice. She wants to make her community a better place for BIPOC queer youth. She is also an organizer with Bleed Shamelessly.

Anika Sanyal (she/her) is a youth organizer who is passionate about educational equity, reproductive justice, and youth enfranchisement. Anika was a Lead Organizer with Bleed Shamelessly between 2019 and 2021, and has worked with the Madison Metropolitan School District Student Senate, Vote16 Madison, and the Democratic Party of Wisconsin. Anika plans to study public policy at Swarthmore College.

Maggie Di Sanza (she/they) is the founder of Bleed Shamelessly and a grassroots organizer for reproductive justice and gender equity. Maggie has worked with Vote16 Madison, the Sexual and Reproductive Health Alliance of Dane County, and the Rape Crisis Center.

After our conversation, the collective encouraged me to talk to Julianna, a member of their high school climate action club, about the intersection of menstrual equity and climate justice.

A Conversation
with Julianna

RACHEL

Julianna! I'm so happy Anika and Amira and Maggie and Amy pointed me your way. How do menstrual equity and climate justice intersect? Do they?

JULIANNA

What got me into the climate movement was thinking about fundamental rights that are not being recognized *as* rights:

The right to food. Clean water.

The right to a stable working environment, where you aren't being punished by things you can't control, which can include menstruation, mental illness, physical disability, if you need to take on a caretaking role in your family. Things that are all stigmatized in American work culture. Period products are a fundamental right for anybody who menstruates.

My high school climate action group is all female, at least right now. We were talking about how it's the basic inequality that fuels *all* of these fights.

Usually, people in places that experience the most menstrual inequality are also most at risk from the effects of climate change. As climate-related natural disasters become more frequent, that greatly drives down the ability of people in those areas to access menstrual products. Mutual-aid organizations aren't able to get out there if there is a huge natural disaster.

I also want to say that these conversations about climate change, menstrual equity, and food and water insecurity don't have to be big conversations like what you see on the news or in the president's town hall; they can start in your own circles. And honestly, I think that's the best place to start.

RACHEL

How did those conversations start for you? Do you have any memories of when you started making these connections for the first time?

JULIANNA

Maybe three to four months after I got my first period, I was talking to my mom, and I was like, "This feels weird. This is so new." And she was like, "Yeah, I know. But you're really lucky."

My mom is Indian, and she comes from a very traditional background. She was telling me how even a generation ago, if a girl was on her period, she would have to go away into a different part of the house, because she would be considered dirty. My mom said this in very simple terms that a ten-year-old could understand.

That opened up the conversation between me and her about all kinds of issues related to inequality facing women. Which is important to talk about with younger people. Like, this is the reality you are going into! You can be prepared to challenge those stereotypes.

RACHEL

Do you think about climate justice in relation to menstrual care products and what we buy? Individual choice can be a distraction from the bigger structural issues. At the same time, there *are* important individual actions, but there is also a lot of greenwashing.

JULIANNA

Oh yeah!!! I talk about greenwashing with my climate group all the time. It's very, very annoying.

There is a surprising amount of greenwashing when it comes to menstrual care products. It might be something as simple as a pad being labeled "fresh nature" scent, which, like, of course doesn't make it more sustainable. But those words, at a glance, will pull you in.

There is of course the issue that pads and tampons are single-use products. You can only use them once, and then you have to dispose of them. They can't really be recycled or reused. I've been excited to learn about more sustainable products, like menstrual cups or pads made of sustainable wood fibers that can decompose.

RACHEL

Okay, either big picture or small picture: What are your hopes for the future?

JULIANNA

I think it would be supercool if there was some kind of government funding into sustainable period products, and if those start to become even more prevalent than the single-use ones.

RACHEL

Wow, can you imagine? I know versions of government funding are happening in New Zealand and Scotland. But the idea of the US funding *sustainable* period products? When we talk about green jobs, that is such a great example of manufacturing the government should support!

JULIANNA

I was actually talking about this with Maggie. Like, imagine if Biden talked about this kind of stuff!!!

But even talking about it in a school setting would be a big step. Climate change needs to be a part of our curriculum beyond just a single unit in freshman science. You never hear people talk about the intersection it has with other issues of injustice, or about the role of government regulation and corporations. Instead, the focus is really on individual actions. Similarly, menstruation should be talked about in school beyond just the very cursory look at it that health classes take. I've never heard menstrual equity talked about in a school setting.

If we are going to have a population of informed individuals, classrooms have to take it to the next step.

Julianna Baldo is an environmental advocate and high school student in Madison, Wisconsin. She has been working with the Youth Climate Action Team for two years.

After speaking with youth activists, I was in a daze. Their matter-of-fact attitude—*of course menstrual care products are a human right*—which would have seemed radical to me as a teenager, now seemed like total common sense.

Suddenly, I could see how the society I grew up in benefited in material ways from silence and no one asking questions about the right to a restroom with supplies that they need.

I could also see how young people demanding something as simple as free menstrual care products in their school restrooms had much larger implications. Because once you start viewing access to period products as a right, what's to stop you from asking about the right to restrooms with supplies, whether or not you are a student? And then what about the right to clean water, or nourishing food, or health care, or dignity, or . . .

What if looking closely at menstruation was a way for young people to begin peeling back the layers of injustices embedded in daily American life?

On a high, I decided I should write to the elected leaders of Scotland and New Zealand.

Last year, Scotland mandated that all public restrooms—meaning restrooms in schools, hospitals, courtrooms, restaurants, soccer stadiums—have to offer free menstrual care supplies. This year, New Zealand passed a similar provision, mandating that schools provide free period products, too. Not providing supplies is viewed as a form of discrimination.

In my letters, I said that my dream would be to include their words after contributions by youth activists, "to show that change is possible and that it is coming!" I wrote mostly just to affirm my belief.

Shortly after writing, I assumed I would never hear back and willfully forgot about my query, a strategy that has served me well in life.

Months after I had forgotten that I had inquired, I received an email from Member of Scottish Parliament, Monica Lennon. Lennon had proposed the Period Products (Free Provision) (Scotland) Act, making Scotland the first country in the world to have universally available free period products. "Universal availability" means that you do not have to qualify or prove you deserve access to free supplies. In Scotland, it's your right.

When we spoke, Monica was in her office. Behind her was a poster with a Rosie the Riveter figure that read MAKE PERIOD PRODUCTS FREE. During our interview, I tried to seem professional, but it was challenging to suppress my wonder.

A Conversation
with MSP (Member of
Scottish Parliament) Monica

RACHEL

That poster is sooooo cool!

MONICA

Aw yes, thank you. And this other one is someone holding up two menstrual cups, like the figure of justice. They're not properly in frames yet, but they were too nice to not have on the wall.

Speaking of frames, *this* is one that made the frame. This is an actual copy of the act. Even though this whole thing is just sitting on a pile of paper ...

RACHEL

Wow. I was hoping you could give us a little sense of the culture that made this bill possible. I know you were a big part of it.

MONICA

It's not that Scotland is any more special than any other country, but we were the first to have a proposal on the table that had a clear ask, proposing that we want free, universal access to period products in Scotland. We want everyone to have the same access.

The vehicle for doing that was community. That's where the magic has all happened. It involved people in rural parts of Scotland, urban parts of Scotland, people as young as nine and ten, teenage girls, and people who identify as trans or nonbinary. It's been a really inclusive movement. What's been especially key is that young people in particular have been included in the design of the policy.

It's been about letting unheard voices in our society take arguments to our national parliament in Scotland. And that's where I come in. I'm really fortunate and privileged to be elected to the Scottish Parliament to speak up for people when they are not being heard.

When I was elected in 2016, my route into that was through asking questions. Sometimes we're afraid to ask questions, because we feel, "Oh, I'm supposed to know the answer." My question to the Scottish government was: What are we doing to look at the cost of period products, how affordable they are, and how accessible they are? Those questions hadn't been asked of them before.

When you think about it, it's kind of unbelievable that we weren't having these conversations.

No action is too small. No question is too silly.

RACHEL

Can you tell us more about the community efforts that, as you say, were instrumental to the bill?

MONICA

Well ahead of the legislation being approved by the Scottish Parliament in 2020, people were organizing in their colleges and universities and schools. We had workers taking action through their trade unions. We had soccer fans organizing and lobbying to get period products at their stadiums.

So we were starting to see what the policy would look like, and then the challenge to government was to scale that up.

I was really fortunate. I got to go to different parts of Scotland—for example, to visit students in Dundee in their university, where they had organized to get free period products. That didn't require an official instruction from the government or a mandate or any special funding. They found a way to make it happen. Local to where I live, they basically took away the coin-vending machines at the university and put alternatives in the bathrooms. And they did that in a really inclusive way, so it's all the women's bathrooms and gender-neutral washrooms as well.

We had good case studies and strong examples of where it was working, particularly in educational settings.

We could see that if we support young people, they will be able to fully participate in the classroom. They wouldn't have to drop out of school because they're worried about not having access to pads and tampons. Teachers were telling us that they were basically handing out their own tampons and pads to their students. So we could really see that there was a need in our society. A lot of people were relying on food pantries and shelters for the basics.

And we felt that just wasn't acceptable to be going on in a country as wealthy as Scotland.

RACHEL

When you say, "This isn't acceptable," are there underlying principles behind the Period Products Act?

MONICA

Fundamentally, the campaign was about human rights. It was about seeing the whole person, in terms of what people need to fully participate in our society, be that in school and education.

The other thing to add, in addition to human rights and health and participation in the economy and education, is the environmental aspect.

That came across very loudly in all the public consultation. There was a real appetite for reusable products, plastic-free period products.

For people who want to access the government scheme—take a menstrual cup, for example, or reusable pads—they'd be able to use those products for a number of years, so they wouldn't have to keep coming back. So there are even opportunities to save.

We're still in the early stages, but that's going to be the next part of the policy rollout.

RACHEL

You're really busting the myth for me about scarcity logic. How you can do it right, and how you don't have to take half measures.

MONICA

When we were developing the policy, there were concerns that this could be quite expensive and that there would be high uptake.

But actually, what our experience shows is that the public supports the policy, though just a *small minority* said they would use it and use it on a regular basis. Most people said they would prefer to purchase their own products and have it be their preferred brand. But knowing that it was there made people feel good and made people who menstruate feel valued.

And it just felt like it was the right thing to do.

Because we know that when you put in lots of bureaucracy, people have to maybe have a voucher, or carry ID, or prove income—it creates a lot of admin, it creates a lot of bureaucracy, and it creates barriers.

Some people were concerned that access to free period products in schools would lead to the system being abused. Or young kids getting up to mischief and messing around with the product. If that happens, it's part of growing up that we have conversations about menstruation! You have to create space for people to learn.

RACHEL

I've talked with some youth activists about the Period Products Act, and I can tell how energizing it is for them to learn that their ideas can scale up! Is there anything you'd like to tell young people?

MONICA

It's so encouraging to hear that young people are taking that action. Young people in Scotland are using their various skills. It's not just about access to free period products, but that it's marketed in a really positive way. The Girl Guides in Scotland recently created a period poverty badge. At school assemblies, young people are talking to their peers about taboo issues that shouldn't really be taboo.

It's about using your voice. Don't be afraid to ask, because you actually might be pleasantly surprised by the answer. And if you can even propose something on a trial basis, on a pilot scheme, and test it out, you might find that your head teacher at your school might want credit for it, too!

Already, in the few months since the legislation passed in Scotland, I've had so many conversations with lawmakers and activists in other countries.

Hopefully what we've done in Scotland shows this is absolutely possible. I'm determined that we're not an outlier, we're not just a one-off. I want this to be mainstream. Scotland was the first country to introduce free period products, but we won't be the last.

In fact, today, one of my colleagues is on a visit to Stanely Castle. And her daughter, who is about nine or ten, noticed that the machine for period products was broken, and she said to her mum, "You know, they don't have period products!" So at a young age now, we're very aware.

Monica Lennon is an award-winning politician in Scotland who changed the law to introduce free universal access to period products. The world-leading legislation and campaign to end period poverty was pioneered by the Scottish Labour member of the Scottish Parliament in her first term, working with grassroots activists, trade unions, and equality organizations. The Period Products (Free Provision) (Scotland) Bill triumphed over many obstacles to achieve unanimous support in November 2020, making Scotland the first country in the world to make period products free to anyone who needs them. A former urban planner, Monica is an intersectional feminist, socialist, environmentalist, and mother to a teenage daughter.

In the '70s, Gloria Steinem wrote an essay called "If Men Could Menstruate."

In it, she describes a world where menstrual care products would be "federally funded and free." At the time that the essay was published, it was viewed as satire.

After all the above conversations, the piece reads pretty differently.

If Men Could Menstruate

An essay by Gloria Steinem

Reprinted with the permission of the author, followed by a new postscript written specially for the publication of this book.

Living in India made me understand that a white minority of the world has spent centuries conning us into thinking a white skin makes people superior, even though the only thing it really does is make them more affected by ultraviolet rays and wrinkles.

Reading Freud made me just as skeptical about penis envy. The power of giving birth makes "womb envy" more logical, and an organ as external and unprotected as the penis makes men very vulnerable indeed.

But listening recently to a woman describe the unexpected arrival of her menstrual period (a red stain had spread on her dress as she argued heatedly on the public stage) still made me cringe with embarrassment. That is, until she explained that, when finally informed in whispers of the obvious event, she had said to the all-male audience, "and you should be *proud* to have a menstruating woman on your stage. It's probably the first real thing that's happened to this group in years!"

Laughter. Relief. She had turned a negative into a positive. Somehow her story merged with India and Freud to make me finally understand the power of positive thinking. Whatever a "superior" group has will be used to justify its superiority, and whatever an "inferior" group has will be used to justify its plight. Black men were given poorly paid jobs because they were said to be "stronger" than white men, while all women were relegated to poorly paid jobs because they were said to be "weaker." As the little boy said when asked if he wanted to be a lawyer like his mother, "Oh no, that's women's work." Logic has nothing to do with oppression.

So what would happen if suddenly, magically, men could menstruate, and women could not?

Clearly, menstruation would become an enviable, boast-worthy, masculine event:

Men would brag about how long and how much.

Young boys would talk about it as the envied beginning of manhood. Gifts, religious ceremonies, family dinners, and stag parties would mark the day.

To prevent monthly work loss among the powerful, Congress would fund a National Institute of Dysmenorrhea. Doctors would research little about heart attacks, from which men were hormonally protected, but everything about cramps.

Sanitary supplies would be federally funded and free. Of course, some men would still pay for the prestige of such commercial brands as Paul Newman Tampons, Muhammad Ali's Rope-a-Dope Pads, John Wayne Maxi Pads, and Joe Namath Jock Shields—"For Those Light Bachelor Days."

Statistical surveys would show that men did better in sports and won more Olympic medals during their periods.

Generals, right-wing politicians, and religious fundamentalists would cite menstruation ("*men*-struation") as proof that only men could serve God and country in combat ("You have to give blood to take blood"), occupy high political office ("Can women be properly fierce without a monthly cycle governed by the planet Mars?"), be priests, ministers, God Himself ("He gave this blood for our sins"), or rabbis ("Without a monthly purge of impurities, women are unclean").

Male liberals or radicals would insist that women are equal, just different; and that any woman could join their ranks if only she were willing to recognize the primacy of menstrual rights ("Everything else is a single issue") or self-inflict a major wound every month ("You *must* give blood for the revolution").

Street guys would invent slang ("He's a three-pad man") and "give fives" on the corner with some exchange like, "Man, you lookin' *good*!"

"Yeah, man, I'm on the rag!"

TV shows would treat the subject openly. (*Happy Days:* Richie and Potsie try to convince Fonzie that he is still "The Fonz," though he has missed two periods in a row. *Hill Street Blues:* The whole precinct hits the same cycle.) So would newspapers. (SUMMER SHARK SCARE THREATENS MENSTRUATING MEN. JUDGE CITES MONTHLIES IN PARDONING RAPIST.) And so would movies. (Newman and Redford in *Blood Brothers*!)

Men would convince women that sex was *more* pleasurable at "that time of the month." Lesbians would be said to fear blood and therefore life itself, though all they needed was a good menstruating man.

Medical schools would limit women's entry ("they might faint at the sight of blood").

Of course, intellectuals would offer the most moral and logical arguments. Without that biological gift for measuring the cycles of the moon and planets, how could a woman master any discipline that demanded a sense of time, space, mathematics—or the ability to measure anything at all? In philosophy and religion, how could women compensate for being disconnected from the rhythm of the universe? Or for their lack of a symbolic death and resurrection every month?

Menopause would be celebrated as a positive event, the symbol that men had accumulated enough years of cyclical wisdom to need no more.

Liberal males in every field would try to be kind to women. The fact that "these people" have no gift for measuring life, the liberals would explain, should be punishment enough.

And how would women be trained to react? One can imagine right-wing women agreeing to all these arguments with a staunch and smiling masochism. ("The ERA would force housewives to wound themselves every month": Phyllis Schlafly. "Your husband's blood is as sacred as that of Jesus—and so sexy, too!": Marabel Morgan.) Reformers and Queen Bees would adjust their lives to the cycles of the men around them. Feminists would explain endlessly that men, too, needed to be liberated from the false idea of Martian aggressiveness, just as women needed to escape the bonds of "menses envy." Radical feminists would add that the oppression of the nonmenstrual was the pattern for all other oppressions. ("Vampires were our first freedom fighters!") Cultural feminists would exalt a bloodless imagery in art and literature. Socialist feminists would insist that, once capitalism and imperialism were overthrown, women would menstruate, too. ("If women aren't yet menstruating in Russia," they would explain, "it's only because true socialism can't exist within capitalist encirclement.")

In short, we would discover, as we should already have guessed, that logic is in the eye of the logician. (For instance, here's an idea for theorists and logicians: If women are supposed to be less rational and more emotional at the beginning of our menstrual cycle when the female hormone is at its lowest level, then why isn't it logical to say that, in those few days, women behave the most like the way men behave all month long? I leave further improvisations up to you.)

The truth is that, if men could menstruate, the power justifications would go on and on.

If we let them.

Postscript

Over the decades since I wrote "If Men Could Menstruate," the subject of women and menstruation has become way more likely to be talked about, and also to be the subject of serious and respectful study. That's partly because women are much more likely to do the studying, and also because a critical mass of studies have confirmed the fact that human beings are way more alike than different. Indeed, in 1972, Ms. *magazine published an article by Dr. Estelle Ramey. It explained that men have monthly cycles, too. In Japan, where high-speed trains had a tragic accident rate, that rate was cut in half by male workers becoming aware of their lunar cycles.*

What needs studying now is the pressure that "masculinity" puts on men to dominate, to measure success by the failure of others, and to resist caring for children or other work that requires simple human kindness. Both women and men are paying a high price for this myth.

—Gloria

Gloria Steinem is a writer, political activist, and feminist organizer. She was a founder of New York *and* Ms. *magazines, and is the author of* The Truth Will Set You Free, But First It Will Piss You Off!; My Life on the Road; Moving Beyond Words; Revolution from Within; *and* Outrageous Acts and Everyday Rebellions.

Back into the Flood: More Stories from Writers & Artists

I've come to understand that *telling* our intimate histories is a way to tell the larger story of who we are, which is always changing.

These last few testimonies bring us into the thick of that most important story.

Fatema

My first period was sticky. I covertly disposed of multiple pairs of stained underwear before telling my mother that I was bleeding. *"I think my period started, but I'm not sure."*

Without skipping a beat, she informed me that it meant I should start praying five times a day. As a devout Muslim who had raised me in a religious community, she saw menstruation as the beginning of my adulthood. Having a period meant a symbolic shift in duty and observance of Islam; she hoped I would begin praying, fasting, and observing other tenets of our faith to the standard that adults are held.

My family's relationship to a larger immigrant community, the maintenance of our traditions, and all of my early conceptions of community and identity were rooted in faith. At weekly prayers, dhikr, and shared meals, my mom found joy in spiritual kinship, and comfort in speaking and hearing her language. Her life in the States relied on having that space, and she wanted the same for me.

But as I entered my teens, I struggled to feel at home at the masjid. Periods became the most convenient pry bar between myself and religious observance. Citing bleeding or cramps, I would leave during prayer time, or not bother going to the masjid at all. Though it wasn't typical to tell others you were on your period, I enjoyed announcing it, as much for momentary shock value as to block any questions about why I disappeared so frequently.

Behind my small rebellions was the fact that I was a closeted queer person unable to see myself in the community that raised me. I did not know that my mixed family's North African and South Asian cultures offer countless examples of queerness and gender variance going back thousands of years; I did not know it was possible to be both Muslim and queer. I did not yet know anyone who proudly embraced both identities without the obligation to choose.

Stepping away for a time allowed me to find my own versions of self, spirituality, community, and identity. It also became one of the many specters that crowded my relationship with my mother. A part of me felt angry that we had talked about what God expected of me as a devout adult, instead of sex or period poops. She struggled to reconcile her image of piety and devotion with my attempts to feel at home in my corporeal form. She picked at me to remove body hair, raged at my handful of tattoos, and refused to acknowledge my sexuality or partnerships. In an argument we had a few years ago, my mother looked at me and told me, "That's my body you're walking around with. It's not yours. *I* made it." Maybe she was right, but what if I couldn't live inside of her image anymore?

Nearly two decades into menstruating, my periods are still sticky. I bleed heavily. Sometimes it feels like half of my existence falls within a penumbra of monthly episodes of depression, chronic migraines, nausea, alternating bouts of constipation and diarrhea, and other period-linked body trouble.

I've found ways to manage my symptoms, but I often feel helpless to hormonal fluctuations within my body. The discomfort I feel reminds me to practice patience and care with other bodies and to honor that a body's struggle isn't always visible to my eye. It resonates with traditions I was raised to keep, like fasting, a practice that is cleansing, often difficult, and fundamentally about solidarity. In my experience, there is another side to the discomfort, the cramps or the hunger, that makes them bearable. Their regularity urges me to not forget. I can understand that what my mother read as an impulse to leave our culture behind was rather my desire to peer into it and ask it to make space for me. And I can also reconsider her invocation of our shared body, the one she made and that I keep, and attempt to treat it gently.

Fatema Maswood is a landscape architect, builder, and artist. They are first-generation Tunisian and Bangladeshi, and make work to dream about a future world remembered from traces. They find joy in working with soil and plants.

Drew

Suppose you were born a boy, but you're a girl. It takes you decades, but you kick and scream your way into a body that finally makes sense, and there's a brief moment when you're happy, euphoric even. But suppose that no matter how often someone says how pretty you are, you don't trust them, because there's still that counterargument dangling between your legs, the weight of all those dream-deferred years on your shoulders, and a past that has its hands wrapped around your present's throat.

You're ten or eleven, look just like your mother, and Dad drags you up the stairs by your hair, just like he did to her, thrusting you into a dark room, locking the door behind him, and all you feel are rough hands. You don't remember anything else, except pain where you've never felt pain before. When you wake up, it's already night. You will tell strangers that your dad beat you so hard you blacked out, but there is no black eye, no cuts, and not a single bruise anyone can see unless they peer inside you. Maybe it's the only time a shock of crimson streaks your underwear, maybe it's the only time you feel what so many girls feel on their first period. But you're different—someone's got to hurt you to make you bleed. This memory hemorrhages, staining everything you touch.

Let's say you make it out of that house. That little food

desert where bills never get paid for a mortgage that's too expensive. Your father gambles away all that money your mom worked so hard to earn. His words and hands and absences teach you to hate yourself. Finally, he abandons you, but his ghost still makes you feel so small that the tiniest things feel like they could crush you. But you don't come of age—not yet. You have responsibilities—your siblings, your studies, and the part-time job you take so you won't be a burden on a budget stretched too thin. You make plans to escape this suburban wasteland. You'll run anywhere—even to an army that'll use you, wound you, and throw you away just like he did—just as long it's not here.

When you put that uniform on, your mother will say her boy became a man, but you only wear it to camouflage who you really are. You know. You've always known. You know when you watched her nursing your sister and yearn for your own baby to feed at breasts that won't bud. You know when you lose your virginity and float out of your body, just wanting it to be over. You know when you marry a woman who doesn't want to be with a man. They send you to war and you kill, and they call you a real man. But when you stand over that body on that dusty field in Afghanistan, you feel like that little girl locked in a dark room, trapped beneath her father's weight all over again. The soldier whose hands are spattered with blood isn't you—you know this, and yet, you can't deny the body at your feet. Something breaks inside. You bleed so many times but never because you can make life.

Maybe you forsake the camouflage you wear and the mask you put on. Maybe you're so sick of this life, you'd do anything to become yourself, even if it means hurting every person who's ever loved you.

You manage. You're alone, but somehow, you manage. When summer comes, your body is new, and you're the teenager you never got to be. There are so many things a second adolescence has to give. First, there is joy—joy at the girl smiling back at you in the mirror. Joy at your blossoming chest and hips and softening face. People call you pretty. You'll make love to dozens in a season. You'll cry teenage tears at every lost love, as if you'll never love again. Boys talk over you. Bosses won't listen to you. Men threaten you and leer. And there will be times when you let people do things to you that you don't want to do, but isn't being a woman in this world akin to being a vessel into which everyone else pours their desires? A hard lesson, but you learn it. Rebel against it.

But there are so many things this second adolescence can never give. Your mother will never take you to be fitted for a prom dress or teach you how to cook or hold you the first time someone breaks your heart. She'll never teach you what to do when you have your first period. You'll never have a pregnancy scare, never have to worry about endometriosis, and never bleed from a constellation of organs you'll never have. But ain't you a woman? Maybe. Maybe not. Maybe you never will be, at least not in the way the world wants women to be.

All your life, you've been taught that the past is a wound no thread can sew shut. All your life, the future felt like a black void threatening to swallow you whole. But despite your scars, too numerous to number, despite the phantom ache of your absent womb, despite those false lessons that'd kept you bound and yearning, you made a life that no man can own, one that belongs only to you. You are unburdened, forever young, and childless. You are a girl so full of every other womanly pain but blood, a girl always on the cusp of womanhood, with so much time ahead of her and forever full—oh so full—of possibility.

Drew Pham is a queer, transgender woman of Vietnamese heritage whose writing meditates on legacies of violence, trauma, and memory. She is an educator whose philosophy centers on undoing racism and oppressive hegemonies through literature and writing. Though she cannot carry children, she is a mother to two beautiful, if spoiled, cats.

Shira

My pads were scattered all over the floor around my backpack. I'd just come back from a soccer game, and as far as I could tell, I was the only one in the locker corridor, unless someone was in a corner snickering. I was Deaf and had no way to know. The next day, I couldn't very well tell anyone about it because who was there to tell? My hearing friends and I had drifted apart the minute we walked into our first day of middle school.

In elementary school, we'd been close. We'd had playdates every weekend. They had learned American Sign Language, and we'd played and giggled through the night on the weekends. That didn't happen anymore.

Standing by my backpack, I knew I stood apart from others at school in some obvious ways: I was Deaf (I still am), and I was a Little Person (I still am). Other than that, I was pretty sure we were more alike than different. But it was hard, at that point in my life, to trust that feeling. I scrambled to clean up and never told anyone.

The following year, I had leg surgeries that took me away from school for five months. My legs were bowlegged at the time (oh, right, that's another difference), and I needed reconstructive surgeries to straighten them. That would allow me to continue being physically active with minimal pain. After a monthlong series of surgeries, I returned home and lived in my family's living room for the next four months.

Soon after arriving home, I received a video from the kids at school. On the screen, I could see students, prodded by an adult to come to the camera and say something. "Hey, Shira, so, uhhh, feel better soon!" "Um, hi! I hope you get better soon!" they muttered, one by one. They didn't come visit.

At home, I was in a plaster cast from the waist down, with a hole in the cast so I could go to the bathroom. I didn't actually go to the bathroom; the bedpan came to me. The day nurse came to my side when I rang the bell and set me up for the bathroom, right on my bed. And when the nurse wasn't there, at night, my mom came to my side.

She also cleaned my monthly periods. The horror! At the same time, it wasn't. In my family, having periods was natural and healthy. So natural and healthy that we never talked about it; it was like eating breakfast, except we talked about breakfast more than we did periods. If I needed help, then I needed help. Despite that logic, I sure did not tell anyone that my own mother cleaned my period mess.

At that age, I did not want to be any more different than others, any less independent. I did not want to have any indication that I needed help more than I already did. I already had an interpreter and note-taker in classes, and I had step stools at home.

It was what it was, but I didn't dare tell anyone.

It wasn't until twenty-five years later that I finally talked to my mother and sisters about our periods.

Asking "Mom, when did you get your first period?" opened

the door to conversations we didn't even know existed. My mother, my sisters, and I started to see that our relationships with our periods were shaped so differently by external circumstances, whether natural design, gentle care, or sheer cruelty.

The conversation with my mother and sisters affirmed what I learned years after I left that school. The society I grew up in generally perceived dependence as a badge of shame. Not wanting to be guilty by association, I viewed help from my mother as an extension of this.

I know now that to get help for something from someone is not an indication of weakness.

We are all unique, like woodwork. The way others respond to us molds our very structure. We can let others determine how we are in the world, or we can personally shape ourselves. We do that by giving ourselves permission to talk, to ask questions, to consciously weave our experiences together, and to share.

You have permission.

Shira Grabelsky is an artist and educator who loves being outside.

Mariana

In English I can think of myself as a child, neither a girl nor a boy. A human child, not the larval state of a man or a woman. As much as I appreciate the existence of gender-neutral forms of "niño" and "niña," I'm not used to thinking of myself as a "niñx" or a "niñe." I like being able to point to my younger self with a word that highlights my stage of life before drawing attention to my gender.

On my way to Mexico, looking for clues as to the truth of my gender, I go through memories from when I was a child.

Perhaps I could dig for other words; the Spanish my grandma spoke was rich. I could say, for example, "When I was a 'criatura' . . ." Now I am old-fashioned, colloquial, and gender-neutral. But that's a word I can't say without hearing my grandmother: *una criaturita, una mirruña.* I wanted to think about my gender, but now I am thinking about the language of my grandmother.

On my way to Mexico, wondering if there is such a thing as a truth to my gender, I go through memories from when I was a criatura.

My goal is simple—I have to figure out whether I'm trans so I can pass on the facts to my mom. Then it dawns on me that perhaps this isn't something that cis people do.

"Do you feel like you're not a woman?" my mom asks when I let out that I'm looking for a therapist with experience on trans issues. "Do you feel like you are a woman?" I reply. "*Es como que soy Lilia. No tengo que pensarlo,*" she says. Her gender feels to her as natural as her name. There's no "truth" to her name, no biological link between her name and her body, yet for her it simply fits.

We have talked about her relationship to menstruation before, but this time, in light of my coming out as *something-other-than-a-woman*, new details stand out: How, in order to talk about menstruation, they separated "girls" from "boys" at both her middle school and mine. How a first menstruation meant being told you had become "a woman" and how she struggled to understand what that meant. ("Like before you were what? A chicken?" She uses the word "*pollo*," which can mean both "chicken" and "child"—another gender-neutral word I had forgotten about.) How my grandma taught her to hide her period and anything that had to do with it like it was the most shameful thing that could happen to you, something I'm grateful she didn't replicate with me.

She tells me one more story about menstruation before I leave Mexico for the US again. The story is about waiting for a period she knew wouldn't come. She had just become pregnant with me, and she was dating my dad but was not married to him like her parents would have wanted. She was worried about how her mom would react and how society might judge her. But, she emphasizes, she wasn't scared. She knew she could make her own decisions, even if it wasn't easy. And that's exactly what I needed to hear.

Mariana Roa Oliva is a writer and criatura from Mexico City.

Una

PEOPLE LOVE A GOOD EUPHEMISM, DON'T THEY?

LIFE HAD TAKEN A NEW TURN, AND IT KEPT TURNING.

I CONTINUED WITH THIS METHOD FOR, I THINK, THREE MONTHS...

TILL MY MOTHER REALIZED

I'D STARTED MENSTRUATING.

SHE FINALLY BOUGHT ME SOME ENORMOUS "SANITARY TOWELS", AS THEY WERE CALLED BACK THEN. WHAT A TERRIBLE NAME FOR THEM!

IT MADE ME FEEL EVEN MORE UNCLEAN.

I DIDN'T WANT TO PUT THIS HUGE THING IN MY TINY PANTS, IT FELT LIKE A NAPPY.

SHE DIDN'T MENTION TAMPONS.

I WAS 12 YEARS OLD. I'D ALREADY BEEN SEXUALLY ASSAULTED BY AN ADULT MALE, SO IT'S JUST WEIRD THAT ANYONE WAS WORRIED ABOUT ME PUSHING A TAMPON INTO MY OWN VAGINA.

I STARTED TO HATE MY BODY AROUND THEN. IT WAS CHANGING, AND I DIDN'T LIKE THAT AT ALL.

NOW MY MENSTRUATION HAS STOPPED...
WHY DO THEY CALL IT A PAUSE? MENOPAUSE.
...I'M NOT SURE WHAT TO THINK ABOUT IT.

MOSTLY, MENSTRUATION HAS BEEN AN ANNOYANCE, GETTING IN THE WAY WHEN I'VE VERY IMPORTANT THINGS TO DO.

I WISH I'D BEEN ABLE TO CELEBRATE IT AS AN ASPECT OF BEING A WOMAN. A NATURAL PROCESS, YOU KNOW?

I'VE MADE USE OF TWO EGGS TO PRODUCE TWO WHOLE HUMAN BEINGS, WHICH IS PRETTY AMAZING!

BUT IT'S A RELIEF TO BE RID OF THE BOTHER, THE TIREDNESS, THE ACHES, AND NOW, IN PERIMENOPAUSE...
WHEN MENSTRUATION IS MORE LIKE AN EXCLAMATION MARK THAN A PERIOD...

I'M COMING DOWN TO EARTH AND...

I'M GLAD TO SAY GOODBYE TO MY OLDEST, CLOSEST FRIEND.

Una writes and draws in a peaceful garden shed in Leeds, England. Her books include Eve, Becoming Unbecoming, On Sanity: One Day in Two Lives, *and* Cree.

Katherine

Recovering from a surgery, Z sends me TikToks of things they know I'm into—new blue pigments, kouridashi, one-hundred-year-old garlic. I'm watching coach.korra talk about using their menstrual blood to feed their plants. A barren, seemingly dead piece of soil, barely distinguishable from city concrete, reveals itself to be a thriving seedbed. I dream. They've captured the blood in a cup, but I'd prefer to free-bleed into the earth.

In my adolescence, my period was announced by migraine auras of shifting color, blending in with sunspots. Blood arrived and the auras left, three days from start to end, a reprieve from the sterility of other days. I enjoyed my period's announcement and arrival, the relief of stickiness on sheets and cloth, the dampness between my thighs. Even then, I imagined going outside to press myself into the soil; my womb unfurling into another womb. But I never did, because I knew the sight would be too much, too strange, too something. Inside, in a room shut tight, my bedsheet a substitute for the ground.

I got my first period when I was ten years old. My mother and grandmother were home; I was wearing a big T-shirt when it arrived. I ran upstairs to them. My grandmother looked at my mother: *Does she know what to do?* My mother responded,

Yes, she learned about it in school. I had. I think I went off to deal with my blood alone.

We had been given a talk by a woman, which lives in my mind as two images. One, samples of jelly that mimicked the viscosity of vaginal fluid at various points of fertility. She played with the tackiness between her fingers, and I loved her. Two, the video of a birth, a baby's head pushing out and the labia snapping back, like elastic, on delivery. I remember other girls streamed out of the room, saying, *I will never do that, disgusting!* I felt awe for all of it, the mess of it.

I was an undergraduate when I first felt revulsion over both my blood and the way I handled it. My period had changed, my bleeding heavier and shorter, gone for months to return all at once, a flash flood. I had never really tried to control it or stop it. I stained things, I woke up in the night to the smell of rust, I felt a trickle down my leg. Sometimes I was too disconnected to notice and would find only the dried crust of a day passed by.

Does hearing these details make you uncomfortable? I got used to that. People tend to be disgusted by bodily fluids, particularly vaginal ones. TMI maybe. That would be my self-conscious utterance if I were to say this to your face. Habit. But this whole project is what you call TMI, the concept of which is rooted in misogyny. And that isn't to say that all kinds of personal disclosure are appropriate for all times, but it is to say that so much of the evocation of the term "TMI" has to do with the need to suppress particular conversations between particular people.

Truthfully, I just needed to talk about it. Instead, I listened, and I overheard. I learned something about the US, being in the US, by the gossip that circled around me from being close to menstrual blood, mine and others. Americans are afraid of blood, of sex, of fluids, of what it means to hold a womb, mine or yours.

Holding a womb is a funny way to refer to having a uterus. But I learned—in the process of giving a womb massage—that it is possible—to actually hold it, feel where and when it is out of alignment, and put it back. At some point, my womb became misaligned. I don't know how, and this not knowing haunts me. I come up with stories to fill the gaps.

The only person who spoke to me directly was someone I had slept with. Smoking a cigarette against a wall, they said calmly, *You should know they're saying you bleed everywhere.* I said, *Thank you for telling me.* There was so much else I wanted to say but couldn't, no longer relevant to our context.

At a party, in the same time period, I cleaned up the blood of a very drunk acquaintance. It dripped down her leg and onto the floor. I didn't think about it, it wasn't gross. I used a plastic bag as a glove. For weeks, gossip ran around that incident, two girls in crisis, *Oh my god, I almost slipped in it!?* We didn't speak of it again; I don't think she remembered. But it had been, in that moment, an intimacy between the two of us, the barrier of the plastic bag standing in to say something like this is intimate and we are still strangers. I think of the midwife in the birthing video, overlaid with another lesson of '90s sex education. Wear a barrier to prevent the transmission of

HIV. Be wary of blood but also "alternative lifestyles." Don't ask any more questions, can't you see what's happening?

Teachers have led me to theory about blood and other liquids that populate my writing. I have not fully, I must admit, taken them up on the reading. I am cautious about the tendency and the desire to abstract. I took a course on psychoanalysis from a Freudian hypnotist. We began each class by sharing dreams. K shared a dream about a large snake; the teacher began the expected questions about male figures, the phallus. *No*, they interrupted, *there are snakes all over Jakarta. Have you ever met a snake before?*

What I know is not abstract; my imagination begins in remaking something. I imagine another responding to my blood, me responding to others. Not by speaking but by tending to each other in quiet, but not in silence, in laughter, in tears. *Have you met me, do you know me really?* But there is another truth, which is that my language unfolds, not in a singular moment of dreaming but in sum, to reveal how I wish not to have been alone in my bleeding and not to have been separate from others in theirs. We send videos to each other over a great distance. So grounded in disconnection, I hope to return to others by reading and writing instead. I hope our words may lead to restored relations.

We bleed profusely. It is the effect of medical neglect—racism, the tunnel vision of doctors, long-term stress, violence of all kinds, gender in all its effects. Blood comes; blood goes. I throw coins, and the I Ching tells me, "you will cry tears of blood for your country." I weep profusely into the earth. All orifices, all parts. I sit in the dirt for those three days without end. Bleeding, naked. In rich, dark soil. Earth which holds me, holds all of us, listens and speaks even when we refuse to or are unable.

Katherine Agard has more to say. She grew up in Trinidad and currently lives in the San Francisco Bay Area. Her first book, of colour, *was longlisted for the 2021 OCM Bocas Prize for Caribbean Literature.*

Somáh

I clearly remember the first time
I found a mess of blood
between my legs
I sat in a public restroom
confused
It had dried thick
and brown
and it didn't look like blood at all,
but something else

I wore my underwear for the rest of the day
and then tossed them when I got home
scrubbed my twelve-year-old hands in the sink
embarrassed
I had been too old for diapers
for at least ten years
so why was this happening to me?

My auntie found what I had tried to bury
and pulled it out from the bathroom trash
I looked at her, mortified
but when she told me
what really happened
what I was becoming

I felt so stupid
for not knowing what was happening
in my own body

I thought that growing up
was supposed to be
romantic
but instead
I wished I were
invisible

For so many years,
I seemed to always get my period
at the most
inconvenient
possible
time.
a ski lift
rock climbing
the eighth-grade class trip
the amusement park with my friends
and every single concert between middle school and college

My mother taught me
how to wash my bloody clothes in the bathtub
with cold water
ringing out the cloth
over and over
until the water ran clear

When my older cousin came to stay with us
she would lay a towel down before sleeping
she showed me how to put one on my own bed
so I wouldn't stain
my only set of sheets

But
I was still never prepared

I thought, maybe
if I ignored it
it wouldn't come

Once, at school
I got a single drop of blood on the bathroom floor
and later that day
found all the girls
laughing and whispering
"that's disgusting"

Why is it that we are taught
to be disgusted
by things that are a part of us?

Last year, at work
I asked an older woman for a pad
she reached into her bag and slipped it up her sleeve
to discreetly hand it to me
and it broke my heart a little

to think of all the generations before me
that were told
it was something
they needed to hide

These days
I consciously choose to talk about it
openly
because that shame never belonged to me,
and I choose not to carry it
any longer

The surprise and discomfort
on men's faces
when I say that I have cramps
that I am in pain
that my uterus is making it hard for me to work today
brings me great joy
because people who menstruate
have nothing to be ashamed of
and maybe
this one interaction with someone who isn't
will break that stigma
just a little bit

I am grateful
that my mother was always so open
about her own cycle

and as I continue to grow
I have learned that this body
my body
made for me by the Creator
is nothing to be ashamed of

Now, I am twenty-seven
and I have realized
that my body does not equal my gender
that even though I'm not a woman after all
and I never had to be
I can respect and appreciate
all the extraordinary things
that my body has done
and can do

My queerness
and my trauma
have sometimes made
my relationship to my corporeal form
unbearable
but the more I learn to love it
and the more I see
the miracles that it is capable of
I treasure its beauty
and its uniqueness
and its ability
to grow new life

Now
I listen
so that I can always be ready

I know that I will swell with the moon
and I celebrate that I, too, am full
and bright
and beautiful

And I make my tea
and I eat some extra dessert
and I lay my towel down in my bed
and I think about the future
and all of the things
that I will create
with this body

Somáh Haaland is a queer Indigenous artist and community organizer from the Pueblos of Laguna and Jemez in New Mexico who currently resides in New York City. They want every person reading this to feel seen and know that their life is sacred.

Agnes

i. The Poet

I am lying on my bed late at night, listening to a poet read a poem. She's crying, sometimes, as she reads. It's a love poem. Or it's a poem about grief, about not falling in love, about menstruation.

> I told them, and it made them weep, and hurt
> Them very badly, that this was womanhood
> To me, the very bottom of it, the deepmost
> And that without this rhythm, I wasn't
> Sure a person could know, really know
> What it is. What it is to be
> A woman.*

Almost a year earlier, I am going to classes this poet is leading online. The classes are important to me. These early mornings are the first time I am meeting a large group of strangers who only know me by my new name. I wear a black wig with bangs, my first wig, a cheap wig, which is stressful, but I am appearing

---

* Reines, Ariana. "Purgatory." *Artforum.* December 29, 2020. https://www.artforum.com/slant/ariana-reines-s-full-moon-report-84769.

"as myself" without apology within the relatively safe confines of a Zoom screen. The poet wears gorgeous dresses, necklaces I love; sometimes there is an orchid beside her. I love the extravagance with which she inhabits her femininity. I feel shy of that extravagance, but I aspire to it; I write about it in my notebook: "I want to wear a dress the way AR wears a dress!" I feel a delicious erotic charge as we gather each morning, faces appearing, music playing; we are here to talk about Rilke, poet of leap and longing. I love this.

And so when I hear her read this poem, late at night, on my bed, this poem about bleeding and womanhood, I cannot help feeling a little sad, a little embarrassed, a little angry. My mind searches for equivalents that can anchor my own sense of femininity. I think about the things I have put my body through, the blood I see when I take out the needle after my weekly hormone injections, sometimes a bead, once or twice a geyser. I think about surgical tables and sutures, I think about hours of pain as someone burns each little hair off my chest, I think about the softness of my new breasts. None are enough. None quite count as what the poet describes as a "sense of belonging in the order of things, / Tidal, a schedule for all grief."

If I am honest, which is to say, a little vain, I wonder what the poet was thinking all that time of my wigs, my name, my clothes, whether she felt about me the way she feels about the man in the poem, who has a "growing desire to worship / The Feminine," which is to say, a little bitter, a little disdainful. In the poem the man who wears tights over his hard cock is a little pathetic.

My conscious mind tells me that I am female in a different way. I construct my womanhood the way a long line of trans women have, really, in thousands of ways, some sly, some painful, some overt, some subtle. But still I find myself sucked back into the logic of analogy. What do I have that is analogous to a period? Nothing, really. Though I bleed, have bled, will bleed, will move through hundreds more hours of physical pain for the sake of that word "woman." The word "vagina" is not the most magnetic word. I could buy myself something close to a vagina from any number of surgeons. No one can sell me a period. A word way more magnetic than "vagina" is "blood."

I stop liking the poet's posts on Instagram. Though it's not out of resentment, more just a kind of heartbreak.

ii. The Therapist

I go on a few dates with a therapist. On our second date, sprawled in the grass in the park near my house, we are talking about sex. They ask what words I like, adjectives for compliments. I haven't really thought about this before. Pretty? Cute? Sexy? I ask them for theirs. Handsome? Devastating? Masculine, but with a softness. We talk about sex, too. What we like. We talk about our bodies, edge close to the question of what language we want mapped onto our anatomy. There's something tender in the asking, something flirty and freeing in the answering.

On our third date, I bring a blanket to the park. Our hands find each other under our clothes. Skin of my stomach, fabric of my bra. I slide my fingers down their back, under their binder. And also, my body slides into a kind of shock. The toughness of their hands over my hips—it's electric, almost as sudden and pervasive as the feeling of synthetic estrogen flooding my body. I feel entirely feminine. Their touch has changed something in my cellular experience of my body.

Afterward, they adjust their binder. I tug my wig forward on my head.

As we are parting ways, their hands grab the flesh above my hips and squeeze. I cannot help it: I yelp in delight, giggle, wriggle away from them. It feels like some true body of mine has erupted from inside the body I carry every day. That that true body has had a moment in the sun.

In the course of the next week, we text a little, exchange voice memos. They are direct and intentional in their care, in their questions. They tell me a funny story about having their period during an exam; the proctor seemed deeply flustered about which bathroom to send them to. They are so good with language, I think. Almost like an air traffic controller. Here is where gender has a space to land. Here is where hope, or grief, or wanting can be given the runway. There will be no collisions in this sky.

The whole thing feels a bit procedural, though. These rituals of language feel so recent, born in the last ten years. An orderly system for narrating transness, consent, and desire. I understand how it serves us, but a part of me still wants to navigate desire, and desiring bodies, without it. What did the Wright girls think, launching the biplanes of their queer bodies at Kitty Hawk? The desire I believe in is terrifying. There is no controlling it. It courts devastation.

A few days before our fourth date, I leave the therapist a message, saying I'm not sure I'm feeling the romantic connection. The memory of that touch is still in my body. But something about their use of language, their faith in words' ability to orchestrate the mad traffic of our hearts, the implicit assumption that remapping words can be sufficient to satisfying desire—it leaves me cold. A lover who would call my body by whatever names I asked them to use, a lover who is that comfortable remapping physical reality with a new set of language—I am not sure I trust them. I am not sure we would be living together in the same sordid basement that feels like the truth I inhabit. Deep in my lizard brain, I know that my desire pulses louder than language, that it shakes off all attempts to satisfy it with words. A new word for my cock is not enough. Nor is any analogy I might substitute for a monthly cycle. I'm all for talking about what we want; I just don't want the talk to domesticate the wanting.

iii. Blood

Language has saved my life. Writing has opened the territory I felt I could occupy, and asking for pronouns has pried open space for me to breathe inside the address of others. Over and over again in my writing I have cast words ahead of me into places I didn't yet know I'd visit, places my body would eventually arrive. I have wanted to weave the wildest skeins of language, bridges, sutures, rags, rages, prayers that can hold together my body and my desire, stretched like Senga Nengudi's sculptures. But when I stop writing for the day, I know all I've managed to do is spill out words. And I want to bleed.

In a note published with the poem, the poet reckons with the hurt her strong instinct about womanhood and blood caused to one of her great loves, a "trans poet of genius." She describes herself as "clinging to the grief of my menstrual cycle as though it were my only true prize.... Writing this poem was cathartic for me," she says. "It says things I no longer feel, or believe. It was transformative."

I am grateful to discover this acknowledgment. And I also now find that some part of me doesn't want the poet to fully renounce her poem. Because there are words, and then there are bodies.

In 2017, my best friend wrote a ceremony for us to perform as part of a night of short plays. It was based on a marriage ceremony. We chewed raspberries and spit the pulp into a cup. We gargled whiskey and added that, too. There were other things; I can't remember. I was supposed to pee but couldn't. She added a DivaCup full of her period blood. The whole thing got shaken in a cocktail shaker and poured into glasses. People shook their heads, closed their eyes, groaned. We drank.

A few days later, we both had strep throat.

Between words and bodies, there is desire. I trust the kind of wanting that refuses to listen to air traffic control. I believe desire when it breaks the language we have made to hold it. And when it breaks us a little bit, too.

We use old magic to make new. I drank some of my own urine on Christmas Eve this year, stoned in a car in the armpit of Hollywood, before I stumbled down the Walk of Fame. I can't quite reconstruct what I thought I was trying to do.

I will continue to compromise and challenge my body. My body will continue to challenge me, to ache, to feel, to cramp, to refuse, to invite.

I am trying not to need anyone to reassure me that I am who I say I am. Gender, after all, is a loose global network that has no home office anymore; we are all working remotely. I haven't worn a wig in months. My head is shaved. Half of what I told the therapist no longer feels true to me. Words start to fall away—or, words flash and vanish like sunlight on leaves.

What would it feel like to inhabit my body without looking to someone else's language? Blissful? Or lonely?

I carry memories of touch and pain like identity papers, like passports, as I approach the border of the land of blood. I would like to apprentice, if that's all right. I'd like an extended visa. And if not granted I'll probably climb over the fence anyway, scratch my leg on the barbed wire, a trickle of gorgeous glistening red that stains my sock.

Agnes Borinsky is a writer living in Los Angeles.

Intimate
Conversations

The following interviews and oral histories were conducted by artists and writers with their friends, their lovers, their elders.

I'm struck by the intimacy and complete openness of these exchanges. Reading them feels like eavesdropping on conversations we normally never get to hear.

Before going on, I want to say: *Thank you for letting us listen in.*

Some of my favorite writers wanted to talk with their family members. They each said a version of, *You know, of all the people in the world, I most want to hear my mom's story. Or my aunt's story. Or my niece's story. But we've never had these conversations before.*

Laurelin talks with her mom, Barbara

I don't have any memories of my mom as a person with a period because she was fully postmenopausal by the time she was thirty-nine and I was four, though I do remember her emphatically telling me to stay away from her estrogen cream. "This is not lotion," she'd say.

On the day I got my first period, she congratulated me with a bouquet of flowers in an ice cream sundae glass.

—Laurelin

BARBARA

I was one of four kids, out of three hundred seventh graders, whose parents would not sign the permission slip to attend a sex education course. I sat in a study hall with the three other kids while the others became educated. I was somewhat curious, and I recall asking a friend on the bus if I could see the book that went with the sex ed class.

I was really mad after I discovered I had my first period. I didn't want to grow up. Things were just fine as they were. Up until then, I didn't really think about my gender, and I didn't want a sexual identity. But I was prepared for my period. My mom gave me a Kotex introductory menstruation kit she sent for in the mail. She probably saw an ad for it in the back of a women's magazine. It contained a short informational book-let describing menstruation and some sample sanitary napkins and a sanitary belt. I got the booklet out frequently and stud-ied the content so I would be prepared for the moment when my period arrived.

My theory is that along with the fluctuation of hormones that come with the menstrual cycle also come some behavioral changes. Around the same time, I was dedicated to the idea of being baptized in my American Baptist church. Baptism was presented as a kind of cleansing and renewal. Well, after I was baptized, I didn't feel any different. What had I done wrong? I kept trying to accomplish that feeling of cleansing, of being without sin. I would redo my homework in better cursive. I would throw away things from my sinful past, like teddy bears, Barbie dolls, etc. This became my obsession. I spent more time polishing my flute than practicing it. I think I became OCD. Although I abandoned the Christian faith, throughout my re-productive years, I continued to carry the feeling that I was not worthy, that I was a major sinner.

Then one day in my late thirties, I got this childlike feeling. Very difficult to describe, but my mind just felt young again. I made a mental note of it, like, *Huh . . . that was different.* It lasted only a second. At the age of thirty-nine, I found out I was postmenopausal (!). Was that feeling the flash when my ovaries said, "I'm off. That's it. Shutting down"? I believe so now. After menopause, I no longer felt the compulsion to strive for perfection.

Postscript

Some mornings I wake up to an email from my mom, who is an early riser and one hour ahead of me in Colorado. "I wrote this after my coffee," she often begins, and then she goes on to write about growing up in Denver in the '60s and '70s, her Baptist church, her lifelong attempts at self-improvement and, ultimately, self-knowledge.

The above came from one of those emails after I asked my mom what she remembered about her first period. I am her most dedicated reader, and I'm always struck by how much her sentences mirror my own, in both content and syntax. Why do we both write in non sequiturs? Have I inherited this line of reasoning? What is hers and what is mine?

I recognize the impulse to baptize one's self again and again. I do it, too. Just tonight I threw away all the rotting fruit in the kitchen in preparation to write this essay. I made a plan to clean the bird poop off my car. Then, I will be good and clearheaded. I wonder if this desire to be pure comes from hormones, or genetics, or the world my mom and I both live in.

—Laurelin

Laurelin Kruse is a writer living in Los Angeles.

Barbara Bolanovich Kruse is a lifetime Colorado resident and retired high school biology teacher. She hoped to spare her daughter from life's confusions but feels fortunate that they can share those experiences.

Cassie talks with
her mom, Chilombo

I've always remembered having a conspiratorial relationship with my mom, or mum, as I would've called her if we stayed in the UK instead of moving to the US when I was little. We've both spent much of our time as Americans missing other countries and, as a result, eagerly telling stories. Perhaps this is what happens when the two babies of the family get together. My mom, Chilombo, is the youngest of eight, and her only sister was the oldest of eight. As the youngest of my siblings, I looked to my mom as the keeper of all secrets—the intractable disciplinarian but also the most trustworthy confidant.

The strange thing is that I think my mom and I are a bit shy of each other. Always seeing who will be the first to call. I think it's because we're so similar. We're more likely to see through each other's postures. Whenever she talks about what she was like as a girl—talkative, desirous of knowledge, a bit worried—I'm reminded of my own tormented feelings of being young and both disturbed and compelled by my own imagination.

—Cassie

CHILOMBO

Well, I was eleven. Maybe eleven or twelve years old, in Zambia—in Lusaka—and it was the weekend before my brother's wedding. I was sitting with my sister, Julie, who was much older than me, a grown woman with her own children. I felt something in my pants and went to the bathroom. Seeing blood, I thought I must have injured myself. Nobody had told me anything, so that's what I thought.

I went back to my sister and must have seemed upset, because she asked me, "Chilombo, what's wrong? Are you okay?" And I told her I had hurt myself. "Where?" she asked me. "In my pants," I said. She said, "Oh," like she knew what that meant. We went to the bathroom, and she said, "You didn't hurt yourself. Let me get Mom." My mom told me, "You're a woman now!"

In Zambia, at that time, nobody would tell you anything. The talk my mom gave me after my first period was basically, "Don't have sex, because you will get pregnant, and I won't take care of the child, and it will be hard for you to be a mother when you're so young and without a husband." There wasn't a sex talk, nothing about what sex was, how it happened.

She was trying to protect me from something that our culture or society couldn't. And I guess the strictness of saying, "I won't take care of the child," was a form of discipline, but also, I was the youngest of eight. My mother had had me at forty; she had been Mom for a long time.

When I had you girls, I tried to give you guidance, but I also knew you would have to figure things out on your own at some point. What was your experience of how I raised you?

I was happy your school had a health class, where they taught you about periods and sex and contraception. I knew you were having those classes, and I remember that was when I spoke to you about the risk of having sex. Getting pregnant young and then your education being compromised. And we always said education was so important. I knew you did well in school, and so I never worried about that, but I wanted to make sure you had the lessons you needed to make it through other parts of life. Like cleaning your room. I know I would always bother you to clean up, because I thought, *How is she going to live with other people if she can't pick up after herself?* So I know I was always telling you that.

When you were little, you would always ask, "Why? Why? Why is this like this?" And I was at home with you, and you would be following me around, asking all these questions. One day, your dad came home from work and heard me say to you, "Stop asking me questions!" And your dad said, "Chilombo, you can't say that! She has to be able to ask questions!" I said, "Yes, I know, but I'm tired! You try being home all day with this!" Well, I'm glad you asked all those questions, because by the time you were a teenager, it was always, "I know. I know." You knew everything! And so we didn't have to worry as much.

Cassie da Costa is a writer. She has an irregular newsletter of stories called Mildly Yours *and covers film and television for* Vanity Fair.

Chilombo da Costa is a public school educator and the mother of Cassie, Miranda, and Vanessa. Chilombo was born and raised in Lusaka, Zambia, and now lives in Pennsylvania with her husband, Chris.

Cristina talks with
her mom, Mercedes

There is so much about my mother as a little girl, growing up amidst the backdrop of the Cuban revolution, that remains a mystery to me: memories lost, blocked, or forgotten. This conversation delighted me with new details from this period of time.

—Cristina

CRISTINA

Growing up, ¿Tú le hablaste a Abuela de que te dió tu periodo? / Did you talk to Abuela about your period?

MERCEDES

Yo no recuerdo hablar con Mami mucho del periodo. / I don't remember talking much with Mami about periods.

Mami era como muy taboo. / Mami was very taboo.

Mami nunca me habló. / Mami never talked to me.

Por ejemplo, / For example,

de sex. / about sex.

Ni nada de eso. / None of that.

I started learning by myself.

Por eso es que yo tenía tanto miedo. / That's why I was so afraid.

CRISTINA

¿Y tus hermanas? / And your sisters?

Do you remember Luly and Blanqui getting their period?

MERCEDES

No.

CRISTINA

They didn't say anything?

MERCEDES

No, ellas no me decían nada. / No, they didn't tell me anything.

Nadie hablaba de eso. / No one talked about it.

Taboo, taboo, taboo.

CRISTINA

When you get your period, do you go . . .

'Cause, you know, in the States,

you have, like, "Oh, Aunt Flo"—

all these funny names for it.

Do people have funny names—

MERCEDES

Aunt Flo?! What's THAT?! ¿Que dices tú?

CRISTINA

Aunt Flo, como fluido?

People call it . . . I don't know . . . Like, Tía Flo?

Or you go, like, "Oh, are you on your period?"

¿Cómo dice la gente? / How do people say it?

When you were, like, twenty-five, did you go:

"Oh, I have my period. Can I borrow a tampon?"

MERCEDES

NOOO.

CRISTINA

You didn't borrow a tampon?!

MERCEDES

Nunca. Nunca hablé de eso con mis amigas. / Never. I never talked about that with my friends.

CRISTINA

You didn't ever have to borrow a tampon or a pad?

You weren't like, "Oh my god, I'm at the restaurant. I need a pad."

¿Hay otra palabra? / Is there another phrase?

Menses? Sometimes menses? In English?

MERCEDES

No en español, no.

Menstruación o periodo.

CRISTINA

I can't remember mine.

MERCEDES

. . . You can't remember yours?

CRISTINA

No.

¿Pero tú sabes sí lo que me acuerdo? / But you know what I *do* remember?

¿Te acuerdas cuando yo estaba en las Girl Scouts? / Do you remember when I was in Girl Scouts?

¿Y te acuerdas que iban a tener una charla para las niñas sobre los periods . . . ? / And there was going to be a talk with the girls about periods . . . ?

¡¿Tú te acuerdas que tú le dijiste que tú no querías que yo atendiera?! / Do you remember you told them that you didn't want me to go?!

Do you remember that?

MERCEDES

¡No!

(*Laughs*)

¡No me acuerdo de eso!

CRISTINA

You don't remember that?

In my memory,

you freaked out.

You got nervous,

because I was, like, eight or nine.

MERCEDES

You were little, yes . . .

CRISTINA

¿Tú te acuerdas de esto *at all*?

MERCEDES

Estoy pensando. / I'm thinking.

CRISTINA

I remember you saying no.

That I couldn't go.

And then you changing your mind.

Y me alegro porque / and I'm so happy because soon after that I got my period.

But I don't remember my period.

I don't remember the talk.

I don't remember anything except you getting nervous and saying no.

It was like you weren't ready.

YOU weren't ready.

MERCEDES

I wasn't ready for you to hear about that.

¡Pérate! ¡Entonces! / Hold on!

Vamos a hablar: / Let's talk:

Tus niños tienen que tener una religión, mi amor. / My love, your children have to have a religion.

CRISTINA

Okay, let's talk about that later.

MERCEDES

Okay, mi amor.

Bueno cuidate. / Take care.

Cristina Fernandez is a performer, writer, and translator born and raised in La Isla Del Encanto to Cuban parents. Her work is often humorous, ritualistic, and in search of the transcendent.

Mercedes Artime Bordas is a Cuban immigrant who fled 1960s Cuba and the Castro regime as a little girl. She lives in San Juan, Puerto Rico.

Mary Marge talks with her aunts Lucy & Susan

The following is a conversation with my aunts Lucy and Susie. They grew up, along with my father and their younger sister, on a dairy farm in Alabama. Lucy is now seventy-two, and Susie is seventy-one.

Lucy moved back to the farm about twelve years ago to help take care of my grandmother, and soon after that, her husband, my uncle, who had been diagnosed with Alzheimer's. Susie's husband died in 2001. This past year, she retired and moved back to Alabama as well. She plans to build her own house on the farm, across the way from Lucy's.

—Mary Marge

SUSAN

The sun was shining, and I had started my period! For some reason I just went running down the back behind our house, feeling buoyant.

LUCY

I would say that growing up on a farm, none of this seemed to be a surprise to us. It was just kind of the natural course of things. Cows and birth and blood and all that just went together for us.

I don't remember starting mine, I just remember her starting hers, and I was pissed off! I'm a whole year older, and I start six months after she does.

And little did I know—I should've been thankful!

MARY MARGE

Well, I know y'all really wanted to talk about menopause, not periods.

SUSAN

Best thing that ever happened!

LUCY

Best thing that ever happened!

MARY MARGE

Your *first* period felt like freedom, Susie . . .

SUSAN

Yeah, exactly!

MARY MARGE

But in retrospect, maybe that was just the illusion of freedom?

SUSAN

Menopause was actual freedom! Everybody says, "Well, it just means you're getting old," and I thought, *Hell no, it doesn't!* You get to quit worrying about a lot of things at that point.

LUCY

Oh, another good thing about menopause is you really don't want sex much after that, either.

SUSAN

Speak for yourself! But if you wanted it, you didn't have to worry about getting pregnant.

LUCY

No more birth control, no more condoms, no more nothin'!

That was kinda fun.

MARY MARGE

What did you quit worrying about? What else changed?

SUSAN

Well, with [my husband] Larry's death, and with menopause . . . if somebody offered me the chance to return to a time in my life, I would choose that time.

It was unexpected, the feeling, but, you know, maybe it was relief about not having to be a caretaker anymore—

LUCY

She didn't have to have any more sex.

SUSAN

(*Laughs*)

No, but I could make my own decisions!

It was wrapped up in a lot of emotional stuff, but it was very liberating.

Just as I felt buoyant that first time, when it all began, this was its own kind of lightness.

LUCY

When you first start your period, you feel very much a woman.

SUSAN

Yes.

LUCY

Well, when I quit having periods, it did not at all lessen my feeling that I was a woman.

SUSAN

Yes! In fact, if anything, it made me feel like I was a more capable woman, that I wasn't subject to—

LUCY

The whims of nature.

SUSAN

That old monthly whatever-it-was!

That, okay, at last, if some man doesn't like my attitude and says, "Oh well, she's on the rag," I can say, "Hell no, I'm not, either!"

LUCY

She could just say, "It's hot flashes!" instead!

SUSAN

If I had to associate something with a woman's movement, like a symbol, menopause would be it. Menopause is liberation.

LUCY

You're gonna like it, too, Mary. The most liberating feeling in the world.

Mary Marge Locker is a writer, researcher, and zinemaker. She grew up in Alabama and lives in New York.

Lucy Locker Crosby returned to the family farm in Alabama after thirty years as a business owner in the Mississippi Delta.

A thirty-year Tennessee educator, Dr. Susan Locker Farris also retired to the Alabama family farm.

Maria talks with her niece Thaís

Thaís is not only my niece, she is also my kindred spirit. We have always had a creative connection.
—Maria

THAÍS

It was Mother's Day. I was twelve. I just remember feeling really weird that whole morning. My stomach hurt. I didn't know what cramps were. And I went to the bathroom. My mom helped me. And I remember telling her, "Don't tell anybody . . . Just let me process this," and then I remember walking outside, and everyone just . . . loooooks at me. And . . .

MARIA

Nooooooooo! That's terrible!!

THAÍS

And then what made it even worse . . . Later that week, I was coming home from school, and I had a bunch of neighbors who were moms, and they were outside, chitchatting, and they were like, "Hey, congrats!!!" and I was like, "Why is this a thing?! I don't want this. Nobody wants this." Afterward, I was like, "Wow, there is *no* privacy." And it's like for your whole life, you don't want this. And you're getting *congratulated.*

MARIA

I guess there are also these expectations about womanhood that assume it eventually leads to bearing a child. And that's not necessarily everyone's interest . . .

I'm curious. We're of two very different generations. You're of a generation that is much more open and nonbinary. You know, you just changed your name; you're considering the multiplicity of your identity and the way you can *change* your identity. How do you consider that in relation to menstruation?

THAÍS

I think about who I am besides that *one* week out of the month.

I'm fairly masculine-presenting. That's just how I've always been.

I sometimes feel invincible.

But a period is like this humbling thought: *No. You may be masculine, but remember: You're a female. You have these parts. And you're going to go through this for another thirty years.*

MARIA

You said you feel invincible . . . Is that when you don't have your period? Or when you do?

THAÍS

Definitely those three weeks when I don't.

That one other week it's like, "No. You are a woman." Not that I would want to get anything taken out . . . but it's just a reminder.

Any other time besides that, I just feel like me.

Like, the other day I had to go to the store because I needed a new sports bra. And I'm walking through Kohl's and it's just, like, all these bras and bras and bras for older women and young girls. I saw all these old ladies, and I'm sure this is all in my head, but I felt like they were looking at me, wondering, *Who is this little boy just snooping around the bras?* And I was like, I feel like I shouldn't be here, but I should, because I do have a chest.

MARIA

I'm thinking of what you said about feeling invincible. It's reminding me of when I was more involved in Indigenous community and Aztec dancing and ceremony. I remember learning in one ceremony that if you're menstruating, you're *already* in ceremony. Your body is going through a ritual, so you were not able to participate in the sweat lodge. Partly, it makes sense, because a sweat lodge is really hot, and it's probably not healthy for many different reasons. But I also really love the idea that your body is *already* going through a ritual. So in some ways, in contrast to what you're saying about that week of your period, I kind of was like, *Oh, I'm going to just appreciate this moment of ceremony in my body.*

THAÍS

Mmm.

MARIA

But the way you talk about not belonging . . . I'm sure that perspective is based in our body politics and how we exist in a very narrow, gendered, patriarchal society. The feeling of being excluded or included is based on that, too. So I'm sure my being "Oh, I see this as a ceremony and a place of power" comes from a certain amount of privilege because of my gender conformity. I'm a mom and I'm married and all these things that are normative.

THAÍS

Yeaaahhhh. I'm just, like . . . ahhh . . . the black sheep grandchild. There's always something new.

I told my best friend, and I told you about it, but I'm so nervous to tell Grandma.

(A long pause)

MARIA

What are you most fearful of?

THAÍS

I don't know . . . She's going to be like, "You're always going to be 'so-and-so' to me."

And I'm going to be like, "If you really love me, you should call me Thaís."

My parents are having a hard time. I feel like I'm being the parent, but I wanna have a talk with them because I don't see an effort being made inside the house. I think my mom has my name changed on her phone, which is cool. But I don't wanna be correcting them all the time . . . It's been seven months.

MARIA

Yeah, that's the piece right there. You want to know they are putting forth the effort. Yeah, you should pull them aside and talk with them.

I work with people between eighteen and thirty, and gender pronouns . . . it just slips out of everyone's mouth. But it's a whole different culture.

You've opened up their perspective so much. You really have opened them up a lot. Probably, they would not have learned this, ever, if it wasn't for you.

THAÍS

This is how my generation is. We're opening up what previous generations were ashamed to talk about.

MARIA

I remember Grandma telling me that back in the day, when she got her period, there were no pads. Can you imagine?

THAÍS

You know in those movies about a long time ago, like a documentary but there are actors . . . ?

MARIA

Like historical reenactment?

THAÍS

Yeah. And there'd be a woman on her period. And she'd be in a tent. And they'd just leave her alone to bleed. To be by herself.

I'm like . . . *that's kind of nice.* She could be alone in her tent or room . . .

Even though they really just wanted to shun her.

MARIA

It was more punitive. But I like your utopic idea. A mini vacay to just rest.

THAÍS

And maybe you get paid for it.

MARIA

Wouldn't that be great. You don't even get paid maternity leave.

THAÍS

Not over here. In other countries.

MARIA

It makes me think about having a baby. And how . . . everything comes out? You're in such an altered state of pain, you don't care. Sometimes I see videos of women on Instagram who are like, "I just had a baby," and they're wearing makeup, and I'm like, how is that *possible*? I was, like, jacked up. I'm just like . . . how . . . ?

THAÍS

In my opinion, giving birth is already a beautiful thing. It's a life-changing moment. I don't think anyone is going to talk behind your back and be, like—

MARIA

"—She did *not* look cute."

I hope Mateo . . . I wanna raise him to be a feminist . . .

THAÍS

He has so many women in his life.

I think it's so weird when guys are like, "I'm a feminist." And I'm like, "Shouldn't you be?"

He's going to have a lot of good talks with our family. We're down for the discussion.

Maria Gaspar is an artist and mother hailing from Chicago's West Side. Her practice explores space, body, and power and has been supported by the United States Artists Fellowship, Creative Capital, Robert Rauschenberg Foundation, and Art for Justice Fund, among others.

Thaís Beltran is a barista and proud member of the LGBTQ community. She enjoys exploring Chicago with close friends, DJing, and spending time with family.

I casually mentioned to all my cis male friends that I was hoping a man would approach me about interviewing his mother. No one did, until Henry, who said, "Of course, this is the kind of stuff we talk about all the time."

Henry talks with his mom, Melissa

I love listening to my mom's stories. She lights up. I've written so much about our ongoing mother-son dynamic in my books, and about how we experience our bodies through illness and disability, but we had never discussed menstruation until now.

—Henry

MELISSA

I don't have an exact memory for a first period. What I do recall about that time in my life was my mother's thoughtful way of explaining to me what I would need in terms of supplies. We didn't have sex education in school, or, y'know, "human development." We just didn't have any course like that; we had home economics, but we didn't talk about periods.

At that time, things were rather primitive. There were special little pairs of underwear, sort of like a garter belt, that you could use by hooking in a pad with strips. It was very difficult if you had to change this pad, and uncomfortable. My mother showed me all the options: the panties that you could use, and the garter-belt type thing with the pad, and then tampons. She was there with me, showing me all these options and making sure I understood how to use them and how to dispose of them properly. I must have felt a lot of reassurance at this stage of life, because it wasn't something that stuck with me as being scary or upsetting.

HENRY

It's so interesting, the intimacy created when it's not something you're learning in school, not something presented on TV—it's something you and your mother navigated together in private and was passed on.

MELISSA

Even when they first started having commercials about tampons, that was radical. "Oh gosh, I can't believe they're talking about tampons." Or for condoms. These things weren't discussed back in the '60s. There were a lot of cigarette commercials, but you couldn't talk about menstruation on television.

HENRY

Has your relationship to your period changed as your body has changed over different eras of your life, after your car accident and injury at seventeen, as a paraplegic, and as a mother?

MELISSA

The injury didn't really affect my period life, except when I went off to summer school in New England. I had been using a wheelchair for a couple of years, and a lot of friends there were vegetarian. The college had really good food, and they had things that we couldn't get in Alabama. Frozen yogurt was new; y'know, granola, other "health food" that we didn't have at that time in the South.

It was all so interesting, and I was experiencing new things to eat, and then I caught a virus and was sick for several days. I lost a lot of weight quickly. I remember going shopping and trying something on and thinking, *Wow, this really fits me so well. I can't believe it.* I wasn't really trying to lose weight, but when I got back to Alabama and started that semester, people were saying, "Oh my gosh, Melissa," y'know, shocked. And that is when I began focusing on food, which developed into an eating disorder, but I didn't realize it. I had an uncle who was a psychiatrist—and that was another thing; "anorexia" was not a word people knew—but my uncle explained, "There is a disorder called anorexia, and it's sort of like alcoholism, in that you can stop before you're in this full cycle."

So he encouraged me and gave me some tips on how to make good food choices that were gonna help me stay healthy, because with my disability, it was very dangerous for me to get so thin. But at that time, which is the reason I'm mentioning it, I lost so much weight that I stopped having periods. Completely. And that's very normal when you have an eating disorder, because it disrupts your hormones and everything. I went to a doctor, an ob-gyn, about this, and I said, "I'm not having my periods. What should I do?" And that particular doctor—it was a male doctor—just said, "Well, if you wanna see blood, you can kill a chicken. You don't really need to worry about that right now."

I wasn't sure that was good advice, but I didn't worry about it. And after a few years, when I just moved on with my life, my periods resumed. And I never had a problem getting pregnant or anything like that. When I decided to have children, it seemed like within a month or two, I was pregnant.

Henry Hoke is the author of four books of fiction, memoir, and poetry. He cocreated and directs Enter > text, *a living literary journal.*

Melissa Oliver is the mother of two sons. She grew up in Alabama and lives in Charlottesville, Virginia, where she works at the UVA Office for Equal Opportunity and Civil Rights.

During a period of my life in which I cobbled together many tiny part-time jobs, I was a studio assistant for an artist. This artist traveled around the world staging colorful performances about interconnectedness that could be performed by local citizens. My task was to help make sense of her rehearsal notes.

We stayed close, and she asked if she could interview her new partner. Witnessing the way he raised his teenage daughter with a culture of open dialogue, she explained, was part of why she fell in love with him.

Emily talks with
her partner, Yehuda

EMILY

One of the many reasons I fell in love with you a while back was because you were so conscious and considerate about your daughter Hero's experience in getting her first period. Hero has lived part-time with you and part-time with Zoë, her mom, since you separated when she was eleven. Hero is now thirteen. Can you tell me about the day Hero got her period and what kind of preparation you'd done as a parent leading up to it?

YEHUDA

Great. Well, when we were together, Zoë and I always had an open dialogue at home about growing up and puberty and how your body changes and how that can be uncomfortable.

Some of Hero's friends got their periods when they were ten and eleven years old. Since Zoë and I lived apart by then, we knew it was within the realm of possibility that Hero might get her period when she was with me. When Hero and I went on trips together to go snowboarding or visit my family in Israel, we would both bring pads, just in case her period arrived while we were away.

On one of our trips to Israel, I told her, "Listen, if you get your period, just tell me and we'll deal with it. You have pads. I have pads. We'll figure it out." She always seemed super open and unembarrassed about it.

A few months after that trip, sometime in the fall, we were at my loft downtown one weekend morning. I had just made myself some coffee. Hero popped her head out of her room and said, "I think I just got my period." And I said, "Oh, great!" I was surprised at how matter-of-fact she was—it made me melt! She told me she'd actually gotten it the night before at a Halloween party but "couldn't be bothered to deal with it then," as she was still wearing butterfly wings and was too tired to do anything but stuff some toilet paper in her underwear and pass out as soon as she got home. I said, "Okay, well, we have pads here," but it turned out that the ones we had somehow ended up at Zoë's.

We decided to walk to the CVS around the corner. Hero promptly called Zoë, whose warm "Congratulations!" I could hear through the phone. I remember her trying to talk quietly in this enormous, empty CVS. She walked down the aisle to have a private conversation while scanning the shelves and selecting a few different boxes of pads. She brought the stack of boxes to the checkout counter, along with a pack of gum. And then we walked back home.

Hero was disappointed by how anticlimactic it all felt, but for me it was rather momentous. I don't know; I was pleased at how open she felt she could be with me. It really meant so much to me. I'm getting a little teary thinking about it . . .

EMILY

You didn't have much trepidation about Hero getting her period. I remember you saying you really wanted to be part of it.

YEHUDA

Yes, because it's a special, bonding, growing-up moment. I guess, stereotypically, if it happens with Mom, it's a given that Mom knows what to do in this situation. I don't think it's always the same with dads. So this was an opportunity, a privilege really, to be the dad who didn't freak out or get uncomfortable.

EMILY

You're certainly not a stereotypical dad. You're open about your own fluid sexuality, and I've heard you talk about having "womb envy" and how you wish you could birth a child, and even have your own period! You clearly have a reverence for the human body. And you are very comfortable talking about sex, bodies, and blood.

YEHUDA

You know, Zoë and I have always wanted Hero to believe in the power of her own body and the sovereignty she has over it. I personally had a hard time as a teenager and didn't feel like I could speak to my parents about many things. There were so many things that were off-limits, and that was harmful to me at certain times and in certain situations. There were moments when I needed a parent and I couldn't go to mine.

So yes, I want to be a calm force for Hero and someone she can rely on. And even though I don't have a uterus or a lived experience of what it's like to have a period, I can observe it from the outside and learn compassion.

EMILY

I love that every time I get my period, the first thing you say is, "Welcome, period!"

YEHUDA

I grew up in the '80s, with boys and men who rolled their eyes and said things like, "It must be that time of the month again." I remember hating that sentiment of judgment and separation, even though it was culturally rampant at the time. I could not have articulated it then, like I can now, but I definitely felt off about it. I just want Hero to be able to celebrate herself in her body just as she is. And I guess I want all dads, and all humans, to rise above these useless cultural stigmas and stereotypes.

Yehuda Duenyas is an artist, an experiential director and designer, a creative director, an intimacy coordinator, and a father.

Emily Mast is an artist and a mother. Yehuda and Emily are lovers, partners, and collaborators.

One of my favorite teachers introduced me to one of her favorite students, who then introduced me to *their* friend in the form of a conversation about bleeding, transitioning genders, and friendship.

Mara talks with their friend Kellyn

Kellyn was the first person who celebrated my transness with me. I looked to them for guidance and comfort throughout my whole process of social and medical transition. Like a younger sibling, I'm always trying to be more like them.

—Mara

Mara was a shining beacon of light throughout the stormy seas of MY transition. They are my brother and my friend for life.

—Kellyn

MARA

Not to sound like your doctor, but when was your last period?

KELLYN

Wow, how did you know that's my favorite question? My last period was also my first period since I started testosterone. I'd been on testosterone for a year and a half and hadn't had my period that whole time. I was feeling pretty good about that situation. After college, I moved to Brooklyn and couldn't get health insurance for a while, so I had to skip my shot for two weeks. I'm in a constant battle with health insurance companies, which is one of the more glamorous aspects of my life. The gap between having my college's health insurance and finding out how to get insured in New York was really destabilizing and scary.

When I finally did start bleeding, I really didn't want it to be my period, so I became *obsessed* with the idea that it was a hemorrhoid. That was probably the only day that I've really wanted to be bleeding out of my butt. Right after work, I called my mom to complain, but instead she told me my childhood dog, Marcia, was dying. I missed the train, so I had to walk home from my job as a carpenter while crying and free-bleeding through Brooklyn. Over FaceTime, my mom called me "fertile Myrtle," because it had only been two weeks since my last injection.

MARA

Oh, man. That sounds like the *worst*. Has your mom always been the person you talk to about periods?

KELLYN

Yeah, I love complaining to my mom in general. Also, she's a doctor, and I've had bad experiences with other doctors before who have made me uncomfortable and given me misinformation. I've had doctors tell me I'd never get my period after I started T, for example. Because there's a lot of confusion in the medical world about what to do with trans people, I think a lot of us end up crowdsourcing medical information about our own bodies.

MARA

Right, I remember calling you right when I'd started testosterone and asking you if it was normal for me to get a period, and asking you when it would stop. I sort of felt like I was having the same conversation with you that I'd had with my mom when I got my first period. So much information about our bodies is just passed down through conversation and through friendship. And for trans people, it's so important to be able to talk to older trans people, or people who have medically transitioned before you, so that you can ask those questions.

KELLYN

Yeah, no one really has straight (*har har*) answers on any of those things. I think it varies for many people. I got my period for two weeks straight when I first started injecting T. I didn't have it again until I ran out of T.

Mara, you've been suspiciously quiet on the topic of your own period on testosterone. Care to clarify, sir?

MARA

Ha ha, well, I had a period once a month for the first two months I was on T, and then it stopped. It was great when it stopped, because my cramps used to be so debilitating. My first period as a teenager was so painful, I felt like something had to be wrong with me, it was such a trip. And then everyone around me was like, "Yup, that's what it's like."

KELLYN

Yeah, that's what it's like! The circumstances of my first period were so objectively bad I'm surprised I don't remember being upset about it. I was fifteen, at a wedding, and wearing a white skirt. While I was dancing, bloody toilet paper fell out of my underwear onto the floor. I actually really liked getting my period in high school because it made my boobs ENORMOUS and I had a special tank top I wore that showed a lot of cleavage. It's funny to me to remember how much I enjoyed that. When I realized I was trans a while later, I wanted to get rid of my boobs and getting my period started to make me feel miserable. I like to think that both can be true. Sometimes I had fun being a girl. I'm also happy being trans, and I'm glad I don't have boobs or a period now.

MARA

Has your period always felt gendered for you?

KELLYN

Yeah, I think it always has in some way or another. Has it for you?

MARA

I think so. I feel like so much of my understanding of periods when I was younger was about womanhood, or maybe my understanding of womanhood . . . was about periods. I remember being at camp one summer, and an older counselor took all the girls down to a little beach to look at the moon, and she told us a story about how we were all connected to womanhood through the moon and the tides and our periods. I understood what she was trying to do, I think. And I'm sure it was a cool, empowering experience for some people there. But for me, it felt totally alienating, and I hadn't even started to understand myself as trans at that time. I just knew that something about connecting womanhood to the idea of bleeding once a month didn't sit totally right with me.

KELLYN

That is so whack-a-doo. Did your thoughts about womanhood change when you started getting your period?

MARA

Once I'd had it for a few months, it felt like a fun secret that me and all my friends were in on, something we could joke about to make boys scared or uncomfortable. And that feeling—of being in on a fun secret or being left out of a fun secret—is sort of how gender feels for me, too.

KELLYN

Yeah, that's a really good way of putting it. In a weird way, it was a little fun to be at work, totally passing as a man, and going into the bathroom to change my tampon. Those moments when gender can feel free and fun are when I feel like it's all "working."

MARA

Right. And then when it's not "working," it feels so bad!

KELLYN

Yeah, getting my period on T was mostly horrible, actually. It made me feel so alienated from my body. All I could think was, *Yep, I definitely made the right choice to medically transition.* Being off T for those two weeks when my health insurance was messed up made it almost feel unbearable to be alive. But it was fitting that my first period on T happened on the day my dog Marcia died—it felt appropriately catastrophic. Bleeding and dying is what happens when you have a body, and it happens to the bodies of everyone we love. Dogs are disgusting about bodies and blood. What I mean by that is they love to roll in dead bodies and eat blood. When I finally got home from work that day and was lying in bed crying about Marcia dying, the dog my partner and I had recently adopted came and got in bed with me. She started trying to lick the blood off my thighs because she thought it tasted good. On the one hand, I wanted to be like, "Now is not the time," and push her off the bed, but also I found that so intelligent in a way, like the appropriate response to death and grief is to consume it and allow it to become us.

Mara Hoplamazian (they/them) is a writer from Chicago, Illinois.

Kellyn Kusyk (they/them) grew up in Virginia and is a writer and carpenter in Brooklyn.

At the senior center where I teach theater, there are two women with a particularly special friendship. Every morning, the younger friend walks across several neighborhoods to visit the older friend. They exchange clothing and remedies, and always poke fun at each other during rehearsals. One day after class, my co-teacher Caitlin and I asked if menstruation ever comes up as part of their wide-ranging conversations. I told them more about the other stories I'd heard. They immediately wanted to ask each other about their first periods and agreed to let us listen in.

Rachel & Caitlin
listen to their students
Pamela & Victoria talking

PAMELA

I was in school when my period started. I went to the bathroom, and I said, "Ahhghh!!! What's wrong?!" I called my friend, and she didn't know what it was, either.

We had to go to our home economics teacher. *She* was the one who told us what it was all about. When I went home and told my mom, "Look at what happened. The teacher explained things to me," she said, "You shouldn't be talking about that!!!" That was my mother.

How did you find out about yours? Tell me that now, Vikki?

VICTORIA

I was at school, and I also didn't know! I had a friend who was more advanced than I was, and she told me all about it.

With my girls, I didn't have much to do, because they knew more than me from school.

(*Pamela and Victoria laugh*)

PAMELA

I know, I know! Tell me about it!

CAITLIN

I was wondering if your relationship with your bleeding every month has changed as you've gotten older. Or after you had children. Or even *not* bleeding in your older age. I don't know if you bleed or not, and you don't have to tell me, but I wonder how your relationship has changed . . .

PAMELA

I find it's changed in the sense that probably about around forty . . . I noticed my period was different. It was a shorter duration. By then, I knew what was going on because I had been to nursing school. But it was still a change to see it dwindling . . . It's not the five or six days . . . Now it's one and a half days or thereabouts.

VICTORIA

When I was in my late thirties and going into my forties, the duration went from five days to four days, and it wasn't as usual. It went on like that for a while, maybe a year or two, and then I realized what was going on. Here comes menopause— it's stepping in!

(*Pamela and Victoria laugh*)

VICTORIA

That made me pay way more attention to the changes happening in my body. Another thing that happened to me . . . I started to get very depressed. And I would cry and cry and cry. For nothing! And the only thing I could do to improve my situation was exercise. When I went to my doctor, she advised me not to stop. She said just keep doing exercises, and I joined an exercise group. And that was the best thing I did, and the menopause just left gradually, gradually. I gained health, then.

PAMELA

Good, good.

VICTORIA

And to be honest, I can't remember when my menopause was done.

PAMELA

Yes, exactly.

VICTORIA

Because I just kept on with my exercises. And I never bled again. Which I am grateful for in a sense. Because at this stage, to be bleeding wouldn't be a good sign.

PAMELA

True, true, that is true.

RACHEL

Do you talk about periods and menopause together when I'm not here? Does it ever come up at the senior center?

VICTORIA

They never discuss situations like this in the center, so we never talk about it. We talk about a lot of crap!

PAMELA

A lot of crap, really.

VICTORIA

If we have a class, then maybe we'll get serious. But with menopause, okay, yes, sometimes we'll make a joke and say, "What happened to you? You get pregnant?!"

(*All laugh, and Pamela claps*)

VICTORIA

But we never had a discussion about when we were young, or what happened later.

PAMELA

Only "What did you bake?" "How is your family?" "When did you last speak with them, and have a word with them?" Nothing else, more or less.

RACHEL

Okay, last question: How would you like to be described in this book?

Victoria Lynch: I grew up in a big family, about fifteen people. My mother had ten kids, but lots of nieces and nephews and they were always there. Brothers and sisters, mother and granny . . . We weren't rich, but it was comfortable. We all lived together. We had enough to eat. We didn't have the luxuries that young people have, but we were very happy. I left my island and came to the United States on a holiday. And I stayed here. When my time was up, I had grandkids here, and they said, "No, no, no, you stay here." So I said, "Okay, let me make a try." And I did get my paper and I stayed here. And I haven't regretted it because I have a beautiful apartment and I'm a citizen here now. I have no complaints. I have everything I need.

Pamela Beckford: I am a free-going spirit. I like my friends. I live in Brooklyn. I am from Jamaica. And I enjoy walking in the early mornings. And I like baking, very much.

Caitlin Ryan O'Connell: And I'm a theater director and teacher living in Brooklyn who also likes baking and cooking for her family and friends.

Across the country, an artist created a newspaper called *The Grandma Reporter*, dedicated to culture for senior women. I asked its creator, Salty, if there was someone she'd like to interview. She proposed talking to her grandmothers. The conversation unfolded in ways we could never have anticipated.

Salty Xi Jie talks with her grandmothers, Siew Lan (Mama) & Cha Boo (Ah Ma)

I never thought I would be so grateful to have talked with my grandmas about their first periods. Mama, my paternal grandma, and I had lived together all my life, three generations in one house. She cared for me when my parents went to work, was my closest kin, and shared a deep and easy connection even though we were so different. I interviewed her the afternoon before everything changed—the following day she was hospitalized and subsequently diagnosed with metastatic lung cancer. Mama passed away five weeks later. Talking about her period was the last story she shared; it was the last day she was truly lucid, her last bow on the little stage I made for her humble life.

From left to right: Ah Ma (maternal grandma) and Mama (paternal grandma) as guests on Eldest Grandchild's Narcissistic Talkshow With Grandmas, *part of my self-initiated grandparents artist residency. The talk show was all about their granddaughter (me), from birth to their hopes for my future. I'd also made a film about their everyday lives, casts of their feet for a project on bunions, and more.*

The original plan was to show my grandmas (and hopefully shock them with) a series of paintings I make once a month with my menstrual blood, while talking to them about their period experiences—important histories I'd never thought to ask about, though I'd collaborated creatively with them several times.

Using my menstrual blood to make paintings has become an intimate, cherished monthly ritual for connecting with myself and reclaiming the taboo of bleeding—a small piece of activism by me and my uterus, which works hard all month to make its lining. It is the perfect natural palette, an exemplar of biological time through its own small evolution. Within a day, shades of red oxidize and become a little brown.

Mama poses with one of my paintings made from pure menstrual blood.

In my dimly lit cave room, with the ache of cramps, I dip the brush into a cup of diluted menstrual blood (harvested from wringing out my cloth pads in the shower) or into my vagina (with legs spread in bed, or standing with one leg hoisted). Brush covered with a reddish-brown paste, I paint mushrooms, brooms, rain, uteruses.

I talked to Mama first, as if driven by a premonition about what was to come. I look at this image and think of how the cancer was, unbeknownst to all, already in her, how she would have a sleepless, breathless night hours after our chat, how she would soon leave us. But here her eyes are still bright and gleaming. The following line-by-line banter (translated from Mandarin) is revealing of our playful relationship.
—Salty Xi Jie

SALTY XI JIE

I only recently realized that I had my period for the first time when I was ten.

SIEW LAN (MAMA)

No! Are you sure?!

SALTY XI JIE

It was in your bathroom. I didn't tell anyone. It only came a few times a year, and I washed my panties in secret until I was thirteen.

SIEW LAN

People in the past didn't hit puberty that early. I had my period only when I was sixteen. We were so shy then. There were no sanitary pads, either. You had to buy rough paper, sand it down, and insert it into a cloth pad sewn at home. Somehow we just knew how to do it. When it got dirty, the rough paper was thrown out and the cloth pad was washed in the nearby stream. Only women did the washing. After giving birth, women put the rough paper on their beds to absorb blood. People these days buy good stuff. We never had such things. And I only talked about it with female relatives of similar age.

SALTY XI JIE

Did your mother explain periods to you?

SIEW LAN

People in the past don't explain these things. When mothers find out, they cook a kind of nourishing herbal soup from *deng goot cao** and a chicken leg.

SALTY XI JIE

Your mother never asked you about it?

SIEW LAN

No. She made me the soup.

---

* A plant known as short bone grass in Hokkien. Hokkien is a language from Southern China spoken by many Singaporean Chinese whose ancestors emigrated from there.

SALTY XI JIE

How did she know you got your period?

SIEW LAN

People know when they see you working on the rough paper. There was a hawker who came by every Wednesday with his household wares, including these products for girls. I used my own money to buy it.

I never talked to my daughters about this, either. They just knew, didn't they?

(*Laughs*)

We've never spoken about this. And they just handled it themselves.

SALTY XI JIE

Why didn't you talk to them?

SIEW LAN

Did your mother talk to you?

SALTY XI JIE

No, but if I had a daughter, I would. It can be scary.

SIEW LAN

There's nothing to be scared of!

SALTY XI JIE

Shouldn't mothers help their daughters with this?

SIEW LAN

What is there to help with?! Children these days are so smart; they know more than we did in the past. No one explained it to you and you knew. Your daughter will understand it naturally; there's no need to explain.

SALTY XI JIE

I wish I had had more help with it. Some people believe the period should be a time of rest. What do you think?

SIEW LAN

What rest? You're not doing anything very physical. In the past some women who were construction workers just carried on. I never rested.

SALTY XI JIE

Let me show you my menstrual blood paintings. Are they nice?

SIEW LAN

How did you get the blood?

SALTY XI JIE

From my cloth sanitary pads. Are they beautiful?!

SIEW LAN

You use a brush?

SALTY XI JIE

Yes.

SIEW LAN

Oh my goodness. There's such a thing? You can't put this on the table.

SALTY XI JIE

Are they beautiful?!

SIEW LAN

Yes, yes. Oh my, I've never heard of such a thing. Unbelievable. Truly.

SALTY XI JIE

(*Laughs*)

I'm using natural pigments.

SIEW LAN

Doesn't it stink?

SALTY XI JIE

No. I do it every period.

SIEW LAN

But don't put the brush on the table—it's dirty!

SALTY XI JIE

This is natural; it's our blood. The same blood that nourishes the baby in your womb.

SIEW LAN

It's different. It comes out from the same area as pee. I've never heard of such a thing. *Yao siu!**

A short drive from my family home, Ah Ma and Ah Gong, respectively my maternal grandma and grandpa, live in a public housing flat. Across the road is the wet market from which Mama bought fresh groceries weekly for more than forty years, and where Ah Ma and Ah Gong used to run a shop. Mama's last days saw her going between hospital and our home; I accompanied her in the ward, and at home I massaged, showered, and sat with her. It was a profound experience to care for her intimately in a way I'd never done before.

Visiting Ah Ma one sunny morning reminded me how lucky I was to have another grandma—an extremely healthy and chatty one, even though she was losing sleep over her in-law's illness. Mama used to just nod with a polite in-law

---

* A Hokkien swear word translated literally as "short life."

smile when Ah Ma went on one of her verbal jaunts. Back home, she would remark, "Your Ah Ma loves talking! She talks nonstop!" I'm sharing our conversation as a continuous story because that is how she speaks—rambling animatedly, guided by my occasional curious prod. Her words fall like jewels I want embedded in my skin forever. This recollection is tears; it is laughter at the absurd; it is the nonchalant wisdom of wrinkles after a lifetime of toil. Worth mentioning is the fact that Ah Ma's reaction to the menstrual blood paintings was quite mild. I suppose I don't surprise them that much anymore.

CHA BOO (AH MA)

I got my period when I was fifteen. It was all red. I had no clue what was happening. I changed my panties, and it was red again. I didn't dare let Mother know, so I threw two panties away.

(*Laughs*)

I was so scared of the bleeding. Mother saw my discarded underwear and exclaimed, "Oh, you've grown up now!" then hurriedly sewed a cloth pad for me. You fold paper in, the kind of paper you use to pray to the Gods. The cloth pad is secured by tying string tightly around your waist and groin. The abrasion caused my skin to peel. It hurt like hell.

How could I know what periods were? We were stupid as hell then. My sisters and I didn't talk about it, either. Educated people today are so smart; they know all about it. Back then, we used to hear others say, "If your period doesn't come, you're going to have a child." We got so scared (*laughs*) and would commiserate with each other. We never thought that if you don't have a man, there's no way you'll have a child. Girls never heard or learned anything dirty. When me and my girl neighbors finally shared our period stories, someone said she was so clueless and scared of the blood that she applied *Feng You** there! She said it stung!

(*Laughs hysterically*)

I started developing breasts when I was thirteen. I was so ashamed of them, and bound my chest by pinning my blouse. We only bought bras much later.

Your mother was studying in Singapore with your uncles when she was a teenager, and your grandfather and I were working in Malaysia. She handled it herself. I never heard anything about it. We had a lot to do around the house, no time to rest during periods.

One shouldn't eat pineapples when having your period; it will cause a strong flow. When I was in my thirties, having had four children, my period came late after a nurse convinced me I no longer needed birth control pills. Big Aunt told me to take stomachache pills to make my period come. It didn't work.

---

* 风 油, or Axe Brand Universal Oil, is a popular brand of strong Chinese medicated oil with menthol and camphor, typically used for headaches or nausea.

Older Sister told me to eat pineapples. It didn't work. I saw a doctor and decided to get a hysterectomy. The day before the procedure, Mother took me to a medium to get advice from the gods. He tremored as the gods came into him. I was so scared. Then he said, "She can't do this! She's pregnant!" He was right.

Salty Xi Jie Ng is an artist from the tropical metropolis of Singapore. She cocreates semi-fictional paradigms for the real and imagined lives of humans within the poetics of the intimate vernacular. Often playing with social relations and structures, her work proposes everyday transcendence through humor, subversion, discomfort, a celebration of the eccentric, and a commitment to the deeply personal.

Tan Cha Boo (Ah Ma) and Teo Siew Lan (Mama) are respectively the maternal and paternal grandmas of artist Salty Xi Jie Ng, the oldest grandchild on both sides. Born fifty-one days apart in 1940, their ancestors came from China to tropical Singapore in search of a better life, where they grew up in villages before rapid modernization. Ah Ma is an exceptionally fit, fun-loving mahjong expert and fan of Teochew opera who cooks her food too sweet and salty. Mama abhorred mess, enjoyed working hard on her plants (especially the giant water jasmine bonsai she tended to for decades), shopping with her sister, and cooking treasured dishes for her family, such as the traditional Hokkien dumpling.

Listening to people talk about menstruation and witnessing live, fragile relationships evolve before me instilled in me a new kind of weight and responsibility.

I had a vision that I was carrying a heavy clay pitcher filled with something sacred. And that my job was to pour it into small cups, which I am doing for you now.

A Full Circle:
More Stories from Home

I thought this project was over years ago, and then months ago again. But each time it ends, I'm carried into a new current.

Teachers from the small city where I grew up invited me to visit their classrooms and lead their students in period writing workshops. Afterward, I invited any interested students to continue editing their stories with me.

When I had asked my boyfriend if he had a period story to tell, he had seemed so confused. But in these classrooms, all the students seemed to immediately understand what I meant when I asked everyone to write about a "meaningful memory that relates to menstruation."

Visiting these classrooms felt like closing a circle. I was in the same place where this collection started, but, this time, I was ready to talk and everyone else was ready, too.

Nadia

I was ten years old when Auntie Flow decided to visit me for the first time. The sun seeped through the blinds and the wind sneaked through the cracked windows. I felt the warmth on my cheek. It was comforting, as if the sun was wrapping me in its embrace. I was sitting in the back of my fifth-grade classroom, toward the corner in my favorite spot: the soft gray beanbag chair.

I settled deep into the crevices of the chair and let myself be consumed by it. My teacher's voice slowly faded into the background. I could hear her reading *The Diary of Anne Frank* to us, but the book in my hand had my full attention. It was called *A Walk to Remember*. I hid it inside my copy of *Anne Frank* and began to devour it. Page after page, I felt myself connect to the characters—I felt what they felt and thought what they thought. Landon confessed his love. Jamie was just about to tell him that she loved him with all her heart, and . . . My mental oasis slowly began to disintegrate as a sudden pain struck my lower abdomen. I tried to ignore it, but soon I doubled over in the beanbag chair, dropping my books.

My teacher rushed to my side. I felt warm liquid trickle its way down my inner thigh. It was scarlet red blood. Panic slowly started to creep in because I realized I was in a room full of ten-year-old girls and boys who would label me as

"Bloody Nadia" and relish in my embarrassment if they saw the blood running down my leg or on my skirt.

I whispered to my teacher that I needed to call my mom. She gave me her burgundy cardigan to wrap around my waist, and I scurried out of the classroom. I stood in the hallway by the staircase. My teacher had somehow made her way to me, flip phone in hand. I took the phone from her, dialed my mom's number, and pressed the green call button. My mother answered on the fourth ring.

"Hello," she answered, her voice as sweet as a glazed donut.

"Ma, um, I need you to come to the school. Like . . . right now."

"Nadia, I'm at work. What is it?"

"I think I just got my period."

There was a daunting moment of silence before my mother said . . .

"I'm on my way."

I waddled to the nurse's office to see what could be done about my downstairs dilemma. I don't remember much of the nurse's advice or our conversation, but I do remember vividly how my mother arrived at the school. She was in her work apron, stained with frosting and flour, and she had bags in her hand. As she walked closer, the bags and their contents became more clear. The Monster High bag she had gotten me for Christmas (I was OBSESSED with Monster High that year) was filled to the brim with pads for every flow and of every color, extra undergarments, pain medication, a bar of soap, and a washcloth. The other bag had an extra school uniform, lots of chocolate, and a water bottle. My mother came prepared, as if this was the moment she had waited for her entire life.

When she saw the bloodstains on my underwear and khaki skirt, her jaw dropped.

To this day I remember my mother's words after she realized I really had my period: "I'm going to need a drink!" I was confused as to why she needed a drink. I was the one who was bleeding. If anyone needed a drink (of apple juice, of course), it was me!

Nadia Gaskins is a senior creative writer at Cooperative Arts and Humanities High School. Her interests include reading, writing, and crying to sad romance movies.

Axel

Not eating at all was the only thing I could do to avoid getting my period like other "girls." At the time, I didn't have words for it, but I felt like my body was borrowed. Not like I was going to give it back, but more like it was something that was given to me and that I got to inhabit temporarily. Like my body was a house that my grandparents gave me. And the only way I would be comfortable is if I refurnished everything and made it my own.

Developing into a woman was traumatizing for me, and I did everything I could to stunt my own growth. My doctor said that because I was underweight, I'd stop developing. So I never ate, and I never slept, because maybe my body wouldn't keep going through these changes.

I was thirteen when my period started. I was in class when it happened. It was March 14, which I remember because it was Pi Day and middle school me thought it was a little funny. All around me, girls bragged about getting their first period, but when it was me, I was ashamed. I hid it from my mom and I never brought it up with my dad. I was embarrassed and afraid. Like this was the gavel slamming down, deeming me a woman. Inevitable and irreversible.

Because I avoided eating, I was very thin and fragile. I got sick a lot, but my parents never noticed that their youngest child was hanging on by a thread. My hair was starting to fall out. I was slowly becoming nothing.

I remember the summer before eighth grade. My family was forcing me to eat more because it was easier to notice bones jutting out in a bathing suit. At first, they lightly encouraged me to eat more, but then they got impatient and forced me to sit at the table with them and not move my feet until I ate everything on my plate. They were worried. I didn't realize it at the time, but this was their way of protecting me.

Later that summer, at a water park, I remember feeling like I didn't belong. My bathing suit was too tight and I felt like I couldn't breathe. My chest had been growing for years, and it always felt wrong. I had gained twenty pounds that summer, and I was finally at a healthy weight. I was dreading the day I would start bleeding again, but I didn't even think about it the morning we left for the park. We had been doing fun things all week because my cousin from Arizona was here, and I hadn't seen her for seven years. We had both grown and developed, and I remember thinking, *She's only a couple months older than me. Is that what I'm going to look like?* I remember that thought made me feel sick. It's not that she wasn't beautiful. I just didn't want to be the same kind of beautiful as her.

I hadn't been looking forward to squeezing into my bathing suit, but once I got into the water of the lake, I felt better. The water was warm, and the air smelled like french fries and sunscreen. I finally let loose with my cousin, and we were playing together in the water and climbing the oversize floats, like all the other kids were doing. I was climbing a large white mountain-shaped float when I felt a sharp pain in my abdomen.

My throat squeezed and I froze. I felt my chest contract, and I jumped off the float. I was frantically trying to get back to my mother before anyone could see. I knew what the pain meant; it meant I didn't have much longer until I started bleeding. I was ashamed of myself, like it was my fault.

When I got to the shore, I explained to my mom as quickly as possible what was happening. My mom looked at me like she didn't understand. "It's no big deal, so what? It happens to all of us." She didn't understand, and her words just felt like invalidation instead of the reassurance she thought she was giving me.

"Hazel! Come here," my mom called out to my cousin, who had followed me and was pulling herself up on the dock. I glared at my mother, hoping the betrayal and hurt I felt was obvious in my facial expression.

"Mom, don't," I hissed through my teeth, right as my cousin came to join us.

"Oh, stop." She dismissed me with a wave of her hand. "Lindsey's just got her period. Can you please take her to the entrance to see if they have tampons?" The use of my name felt worse than my cramps. I hated my name ever since I learned how to say, "My name is Lindsey." Even when I was a child, when people asked what my name was, I'd give them a different name. "Sky," I'd say. "My name is Sky." Before I could process why it hurt to hear my own name, Hazel looped her arm into mine.

"Let's go." She smiled at me warmly, but I still felt humiliated. I felt like I barely knew her, and now she was helping me take care of my period. Her kindness made it easier for me to keep walking with her. My cousin had a sunburn on the tops of her shoulders and across her cheeks and nose. I remember wondering if I was going to burn, too, trying to get my mind anywhere but what was going on between my legs. We rushed the rest of the way there, and she stood outside the bathroom stall, pushing quarters into a tampon dispenser. I bit my lip, trying not to cry, but I had never used a tampon before, so I was scared. She passed it to me under the stall, and my eyes started to well with tears.

By the time I left the stall, I had made sure to wipe my tears from my face and get control of my breathing. I felt wrong all over and the bathing suit felt tighter than it had before. I felt naked and exposed. I felt like everyone was looking at me, like everyone knew I was on my period. I know now that it was paranoia, but at the time I felt like everyone was in on the joke. The misfit on her period.

Almost four years later, I've been out as a transgender boy for more than a year. My parents still don't understand, but they've started the slow process of accepting me. I still struggle with my period when it comes, but it's easier to go through now that I have a support system that respects me and my identity. Figuring out who I was took a lot out of me, but I don't regret anything. I'll never regret finding myself. And I know I'm not done yet, but at least I have a start.

Axel Gay is a junior in high school who has been working toward getting to know himself for years. He's recently come out as transgender to his friends and family.

Jordyn

I was nine years old when I got my first period. It was in the middle of a church service, and I went to find my aunt so she could help.

"Uhhh, Auntie . . . I just went to the bathroom, and there's red stuff in my panties."

Her laugh gave me reassurance that I wasn't dying. She explained to me that once we get older, we have a cycle that causes our private part to bleed. She taught me how to put on a pad and called my dad to come pick me up.

In the car, all I could hear was silence. I wondered why. Did he talk to my sisters when it came to their periods? How is he with my mom when she has her period? Why does he not want to talk about this situation? The awkwardness was as thick as a wall.

"My baby's a woman now!" my mom yelled as I walked into the house. Right away, my mom wanted to know my whole thought process and reaction to seeing the blood in my panties. She wanted to talk, talk, talk, and talk. Way different than my dad and aunt.

She then proceeded to hand me a pink sparkly bag that had an extra pair of panties, pads, and liners. She explained what the difference was between a pad and a liner. She also told me that it was important to keep the bag with me at all times, because there might be a time when my period sneaked up on me and I'd need backup, or one of my friends might. My mom explained the importance of girls having one another's backs. Having something as simple as a pad could let another girl know she was not alone in the world. She would want another girl to help me if I was in that situation and did not want me to be alone.

Jordyn McBride is currently a senior in college, studying marketing and management.

Piper

"Congratulations," my mom says as she turns out the light for me to go to sleep. My stomach turns at her words.

"Why?" I snap. "It's just an inconvenience."

She shrugs, at a loss, and gently shuts the door. What I don't say is that this is so much more than an inconvenience. This is painful, but not because of any cramps. This hurts because it's so wrong. It was never supposed to happen, yet here I am bleeding, and people seem to think it's something I should be happy about.

At least I can still dress up in clothes that feel right. Maybe a flannel over a baggy black T-shirt and light-wash jeans will snap me back into my reality. But my attempt is quickly thwarted.

"Are you sure you want to wear those light pants?"

I feel like throwing up.

Is there anything that periods don't take over and control? Or will they keep infesting everything I think is safe for the rest of my life? And even if I'm not bleeding now, it could start any minute. How much longer do I have to enjoy this freedom?

I had always been told that periods were a milestone, the beginning of a new chapter of life, but I'm in mourning. I'm mourning over being able to live carefree, go to swim practice every night, and move through life without the fuzzy buffer of dissociation. Periods are a constant stressor on my mind, simultaneously, paradoxically pulling me apart and compressing me, widening the rift between mind and body and shrinking me to a fraction of myself.

I grew up assuming that female puberty wouldn't apply to me. It was completely absurd to me to think that I would ever become a woman and mature like other girls. I thought I was somehow exempt, like if I denied biology intensely enough, I could push its effects away with sheer willpower.

Despite the black hole of periods swallowing me up for years, I was eventually spit back out on the other side. Periods were an evil that ended when I was able to go on testosterone.

Looking back, I can say I was never better, wiser, or stronger for having endured periods. Bleeding doesn't always make you more compassionate or intelligent or self-aware; sometimes it just makes you suffer.

There's really no moral to this story. There's no happy ending where I learn to live with periods and accept them as a part of myself. They're just not. Periods were horrifying every time they arrived until I stopped playing host for them. The trauma of being repeatedly reminded that your body, both inside and out, does not belong to you and is not under your control isn't something that just resolves itself.

In my short sixteen years of life, I've seen the stigma surrounding the topic of periods wither and crumble. Though it's positive that people are able to speak freely about and even celebrate their periods, that positivity should never be a requirement. I'm allowed to hate what happened to me as much as others are allowed to enjoy their periods. I don't have to live with pain just because it's natural. There's always room to change what you simply can't, and shouldn't have to, live with.

Piper Zschack is a junior in high school and still a work in progress, but trying his best.

In some of the classrooms I visited, teachers shared their own stories as a way to invite their students to go to a vulnerable place. I asked if they would be willing to share their stories with us, too.

Mindi

My period ended just as my daughter's began. I had her late, at forty. She has newly acquired boobs where her chest used to be. She has all the hairy parts I am losing. She has a life ahead of her to plan, be surprised by, replan, and remember. Her options are open and ahead of her, and this is a pleasure for me to behold.

I am in a different stage. I have my gains and my losses. Bull's-eyes, misses, and near misses to reflect upon. I have more memories behind me than ahead of me, I suppose.

Entering menopause, I feel a deeper connection to my ancestors who had to leave their homeland. I am a refugee now. After all, women leave so much behind when our periods are gone. Yes, we leave behind the strife and the pain. But we also leave a large part of our societal worth, our sense of identity. And who is there to welcome us older women as we arrive on the shores of menopause, with our lack of estrogen, our saggy skin, our dysregulated body temperatures, our graying hair? America does not have a seat of honor for its aging women. It doesn't always even have a seat. Sometimes we must sit our creaky bones down, right there in the dirt.

I wandered for a long time. I was dehydrated; vitamins left too quickly and weight gathered at the center of me, where my baby had once been. I had given all I could with this body to nurture the next generation. What was my reward? Free-floating anxiety? Itchy skin? A newfound invisibility and ir-relevancy to either fight against or embrace?

The evolutionary idea that a human's prime directive is to procreate leaves us without a clear purpose. "What IS the purpose of the woman without a period?" we ask ourselves as we struggle to learn a new language so we can be heard, wear clothes appropriate for our age so we can be seen, and scrabble through our baggage for any kind of currency to use here in the world that is the same but seems so different now. No one wants to talk about menopause. It feels like an ugly word with negative connotations but only, I think, because it remains under-discussed.

I'd like to say I am happy here now. And I think I will be able to say that eventually. Right now, I'm tired from the long voyage, from the lack of journeying companions, from the need to redefine my body and my cultural relevance. I think I will like the lack of catcalling, the worry of an unwanted pregnancy or unwanted sexual advances, the cramps and the constant buying of supplies, and the freedom I had all along (but didn't fully realize) to dress, act, think, and talk however I wanted. I do look forward to the wisdom, the simplicity, the lessened sense of drama in this new place.

As a descendant of refugees, I have heard storied whispers along the way. I knew enough to sew seeds into the lining of my coat before I left my youth. They are heirloom seeds. Seeds of wisdom, love, belief. Each contains multitudes. The contin-uation of what was and should be.

I have already begun planting them, here and there, in the soil around my daughter, my students, myself, and I've even sewn them here, in the words I write to you now.

Mindi Rose Englart is a writer, artist, high school teacher, and, most recently, founder of the Single Mothers Discount Card.

Marian

Prologue

I knew about periods early on because I have a sister five years older. There were no secrets. I saw the pain each month, bore the brunt of the mood changes, the pads, and saw the bloody sheets. I knew this was no fun and that I should expect the pain each month when it happened to me. My mother said, "It is your friend, because when it doesn't happen, it is not your friend." When I finally got my period, I remember everything feeling amplified because my sister and I would cycle pretty close to each other. It felt like chaos in my house.

Friend's Secret

My "friend" has a secret that makes me dance through my apartment.

My LOVE is coming tonight, and I will reveal my friend's secret.

My friend has not been a friend for two months (no period for two months, positive test)!

It is the FIRST time I am happy about this.

My LOVE arrives and makes me feel like a puppy dog (tail wagging so hard it makes my body shudder). We kiss, we greet, we talk, we eat.

I remember being so happy I thought I might EXPLODE, with my friend's secret and my tail wagging.

My LOVE tells me, "I have something to tell you." I think, *Engagement? Marriage?*

I remember the words "old girlfriend," "pregnant," "before you came back home."

Sadness and grief, like honey, dripped down my head, onto my face, and down my body.

I kept my secret, and later, tears and blood flowed like a river.

Marian Evans is an assistant professor in the Department of Public Health and Women's and Gender Studies at Southern Connecticut State University. She has taught a Women's Health and Women's Health Consciousness course for sixteen years. She is also a trained ob-gyn who brings period experiences and knowledge with her into the classroom, but her students have taught her so much more.

Had any of my teachers ever talked to me about a personal experience of menstruation?

When I think about how challenging it is to grow, and to grow into a changing body, it seems striking that no adult said to me, "Listen, I went through this, too" or "I'm in a version of it now" or even just "Change is constant, honey."

Now that the circle was closed, I decided this book was done.

Of course, that very same week, I heard a story from a friend about a time when a tampon got stuck in her vagina. Her husband tried to use his headlamp to help fish it out, but to no avail. She ended up having to "give birth" to it; it was the only way! A few days later, a couple told me about one of the first times they slept together. They'd been at a Halloween party and, later that night, found themselves tangled in reddish-brown sheets. *This must be our gory makeup*, they each thought. In fact, it was *both* their periods! As they spoke, they seemed deeply in love.

Hearing these stories back-to-back felt like a sign. A reminder of the impossibility, the absurdity of hearing everything, of sharing everything, because these stories are everywhere and in everyone. And how for every story that is shared, there are vastly more that remain unwritten and unsaid.

But naturally, when I thought the project was really over, there were a few more trickles that came as a surprise.

Months after I visited her classroom, the high school teacher wrote to me. She explained that when I had led my writing workshops, her daughter had also been home, attending school remotely, and had quietly followed along. She had finished her story and wondered if she could share it with me.

Lily

When one of my friends gets their first period, I make them a cake. I have done this four times now. I start by making a red velvet cake (from a box). I then add red frosting and many decorations, such as berries, tiny umbrellas, and candles they can blow out to make a wish.

I make period cakes simply because no one else will.

From a very early age, I learned how boys react to periods, like how they yelled "TMI" at me just for telling the PE teacher that I couldn't participate in gym. Or when I dropped my pad on the floor while I was cleaning out my locker and they acted like it was a bomb.

The worst thing occurred in seventh grade during a sex ed class. The first problem was that the teacher did not separate genders. We all sat in one classroom, learning about wet dreams, boobs, and periods. It was the most uncomfortable environment you could think of. The boys all sat together, making jokes, laughing in the corner. And the girls sat silent.

I, myself, was paralyzed in my chair because I couldn't bear to look up. It was as if I was on a ledge very high up and was afraid to move even my eyes. We were watching a video that had young teens saying the cheesiest lines to get the point across. I had *no* respect for those actors.

I'd like to make clear I am a very open person; very little is off the talking table for me. But apart from the boys joking their asses off, I assume as a coping mechanism, the information on periods WAS JUST PLAIN WRONG! Also it was sexist.

In one scene, we were told that every woman produces twelve tablespoons of blood each month. Another scene had a boy saying his sister was too emotional and dramatic. But the worst one was when they said that girls wouldn't feel pain during their period and how they could still do gym and partake in strenuous physical activity.

It was at that point I looked promptly at the screen and could not believe HE, our health teacher, had projected a film that so bluntly spewed a lie. I can only imagine what somebody would have thought looking at my face. I just know I had a flat-out flabbergasted look on it.

I thought many things. Number one: how I wished the boys weren't there. Not because I don't think we should learn about each other's biology but because they would think that women use their periods only as excuses. They would think girls are exaggerating or overly emotional or weak for feeling pain because *school*, the place where we *learn*, had told them the opposite.

Number two: I was concerned girls would be led astray with this misleading information. Many of the girls didn't have their periods yet. And when they did, they would think there was something wrong with them for having more or less blood than in the video or for having cramps.

The third thing that bothered me was that the video said girls should attend PE classes. This made me so angry, because here is this man, who probably doesn't know anything about periods, showing us this video, which was sent from the school district, because that's his job. And we're not actually *talking* about periods, because that's the culture, and instead the video, because it's from the school district, is overstepping its power to tell us we have to go to GYM?!

When I got home, I asked my mom why the video told everyone that periods weren't painful, and she said they probably didn't want to alarm any of the girls. I thought that was so ignorant and stupid. If they didn't want to worry girls, they should have told the truth; otherwise, the girls would inevitably end up being really scared when they got their periods.

We all know womanhood can be very challenging; that's why it's good to start it off with a sweet taste of support and a little cream cheese frosting.

Lily Grace Sutton is a rising high school sophomore. Her hobby is keeping up with relationships. Her interests are animals and fashion.

On the phone with Lily, after she read her piece aloud, I asked her about her plans for the weekend. She was getting her ears pierced with her best friend.

"That's so exciting! Is there a reason you're getting your ears pierced now?" I asked.

"Oh, no, I already have my ears pierced," she clarified. "I'm getting my *cartilage* pierced."

"Ohhhhh," I said, the power dynamic shifting completely.

Being a teenager, it occurred to me, was just as hardcore as giving birth and dying.

My mom found a letter in the attic and sent me a photo of the first page. It was addressed to her mother, my grandmother. My mom was writing because she had discovered something in her underwear that was brown and reddish. "But not to worry," she wrote, it wasn't her period! There was a follow-up letter, written a month later, explaining that, though it was hard to believe, this was in fact her period!

The letter, written a few years before my grandmother died, was filled with a buoyancy and ease I had never experienced with my mother. Encountering this part of her made me cry.

When I was a teenager, I thought my life was my life and my body was my body. Now I see how I am a reaction to my mother, and how she is a reaction to her mother, and how there is a thread between us that is still in motion, that is still evolving the more we learn and the more we heal. History doesn't go away, it seemed to me as I looked closely at my mother's teenage cursive, it just changes.

There is only one woman of my tante Nina's generation who is still alive. For years, I have avoided interviewing her. Archiving anything she says feels like an acceptance of the end.

One morning, when I was out for a walk, I decided to call my tante Odette right then and there. Maybe if I did it in the spur of the moment, I thought, an interview wouldn't feel so final. I scribbled notes from our conversation in French on a spare envelope. Still, I cried afterward.

A Conversation
with Tante Odette

ODETTE

I know immediately what I want to tell you. I want to tell you about the times when my period *left*, due to trauma.

The first time was when I was fifteen years old and my father died. We were in the hospital, and he told me to go home. He didn't want me to see him dying, and I took it personally.

I couldn't be a woman anymore.

How do I explain? I felt utterly rejected—rejected to the point of my *humanity*.

That was the first time my period left.

At the time, we talked about nothing. This was 1945, and we were leaving the war. We didn't talk about ourselves. We didn't complain. We'd all been through so much tragedy. But trauma . . . it seeps into the body.

RACHEL

Did you understand the connection between trauma and the body at the time?

ODETTE

At that age, no. I viewed it as a punishment. I took it as a sign of my culpability, for my dad's illness.

The second time, it was also connected to guilt. I was twenty-one. Three friends and I were hiking in the mountains. A boulder fell and hit my three friends, killing them.

But I was untouched. *Why me, why me?!* I was ten meters away.

One of my friends was six months pregnant.

It's one of those events that cuts your life in half: there's a before and an after. I lost my period for two to three years after that.

RACHEL

I've heard that story before. But I didn't know your period had gone away after. When did you start understanding the way trauma affects the body? Was it after you became a doctor?

ODETTE

After I became a doctor, yes.

And right now! Right now, I'm making the link.

The culpability, the unbearability of existing . . .

And now, again, at this phase of my life, I can no longer be a woman, either.

There's a feeling of *perte*—of loss.

In French, we say, "*J'ais des pertes*," to talk about the spotting around menopause.

Now that I can't see or write, it feels good to talk.

Keeping it all inside is a kind of poison.

Odette Waks is a ninety-one-year-old practicing psychoanalyst living in Paris. She describes herself as a doctor and psychiatrist who wants to understand "the source and the meaning of our symptoms, which is the subconscious."

Out of the blue, months after we'd been in touch, a friend emailed me:

I feel inclined to share this, even if it doesn't aid the project in any way. My father passed away when I was 12, and I got my first period just a month after. My mom never got hers again—she went into early menopause. I've always found this interesting, how grief has so much of a role to play in bodily changes . . .

love,
sim

All these stories of death and how the body responds.

I wanted to talk with a scientist who could tell me about the relationship between emotions and blood.

The New York Times had just published an article about how little is known about menstruation. The article was a response to the dramatically altered periods that people reported experiencing following their COVID-19 vaccinations. There were delayed periods, heavier periods, even periods that returned after menopause. Though public health officials assured everyone there were no lasting consequences of vaccination, they couldn't *technically* say whether or how the vaccine had affected anyone's menstrual cycle. This was because the drug trial had completely overlooked menstrual side effects. As the article explained, ignoring menstrual variation is commonplace. Medical researchers have historically regarded menstruation as a confounding variable, too unwieldy to make sense of, like static on the radio. But it was time—past time, the article suggested—to study menstruation and heed its signs.

In a stolen hour at the hospital, I spoke to one of the article's authors, Dr. Alice Lu-Culligan, who studies pregnancy and the immune system. I asked whether it was possible, given the state of menstrual research, to understand why so many stories about blood seem fateful.

A Conversation
with Alice

RACHEL

When I learned about your research, I thought, *I can't believe it doesn't exist already!* How do you make sense of this?

ALICE

It's a historical problem. Women's and all minorities' health have been underserved for a long time, partly due to the lack of diversity in the sciences. Most researchers in the past were men who wielded great power and freedom to study whatever they thought was most important. Unsurprisingly, this was not very inclusive of the experiences of women or minorities.

But topics like pregnancy and menstruation are also really difficult and complex phenomena to study. There are a lot of ethical issues in play when you are talking about studying minors or pregnant women. Then there's also the difficulty of studying women when everyone has a different cycle, and every woman at any given time is in a different part of that cycle. It's not necessarily easy to determine what standards we should use to track and measure these complex kinds of data. But that's also because we haven't given a lot of thought to creating those standards.

On top of all that, most mammals don't menstruate, which makes it difficult to study in a lab.

If we're taking an honest assessment, it's clear we just don't have the hundreds of years of foundational knowledge under us like we have in other fields.

That being said, there have been breakthroughs even in just the past few years, in terms of, for example, creating a biological model that can mimic menstruation.

RACHEL

Can you tell us how being behind in studying pregnancy and menstruation impacts people? Why does this gap in research matter?

ALICE

A lot of doctors and researchers don't want to talk about menstruation, partly because they might feel embarrassed, but *also because they don't know a lot about it*. Sure, they know the basics in terms of the main hormones regulating the cycle. But there are a lot of things about our periods and why they vary so much between women that can't be explained easily by our current state of knowledge. So it becomes an easy topic to avoid.

This stigma might stop people from talking to their doctors about important issues with their period, which is problematic because your menstrual patterns can be a part of the overall picture of your health. Or it could even prevent people from sharing regular updates about their periods.

It also means that during research trials, participants might not bring up their period if it is affected.

RACHEL

Could we talk about the development of the COVID-19 vaccine, and why overlooking menstruation led to a lot of preventable confusion?

ALICE

For the COVID-19 vaccine, in a way there was nothing unusual about the structure of the trial. They simply did what almost every other clinical trial does, which is to completely ignore the menstrual cycle. And you know, to be fair, we were in a global emergency, and the primary goal of the study was not connected to periods.

But . . . that gap in knowledge *did become an issue* when some women started to report that they were having these huge changes to their periods following the vaccine. Most women didn't experience a change, but there was enough discussion around it that it became a question and also a source of fear for some.

We're talking about women of all ages, backgrounds, and medical histories who have different anecdotal reports of what they're experiencing following vaccine, whether it's heavier bleeding, a skipped period, or postmenopausal bleeding.

At the heart of it, no one doubts that these women experienced a change in their periods. But without a properly designed study, we can't know if there is a real association.

So we continue to be in this bind.

We also don't actually have much data regarding menstruation from other trials to understand if this is likely.

RACHEL

Taking a quick step back: Can you give some historical context on clinical trials, and how we find ourselves here?

ALICE

Throughout most of history, clinical trials typically excluded the participation of women, especially women in their childbearing years. In the US, it wasn't until 1993 that it was formalized that women had to be included as a part of clinical trials. Which means that before then, most drugs were being tested only on men.

It wasn't until Congress signed into law that you have to have a representative population—which includes gender and also ethnic backgrounds—in our medical trials and preapproval studies that things changed.

That's not very long ago. It's obviously super problematic that inclusivity wasn't the norm until quite recently in history.

It wouldn't be that hard to implement some small changes, though. It would be great if clinical trials approached periods as just another potential area for side effects. We could simply ask people to note if any striking or unusual changes happen. Not as a potential reason for panic but as a nonspecific piece of data that could be useful.

Especially in an age of misinformation, these type of data can really make a difference to people who *do* experience side effects. Because maybe it's a *normal expected* response, and there might not be anything to worry about. To be clear, even if there *are* period changes following a vaccine, do I think they are definitively harmful to a woman's biology, health, or fertility? No, that's certainly not where my mind goes first. But the danger is more that if people don't understand that this is a change that *could* happen, that's when uncertainty and fear can start to create myths and rumors. And of course people might start to mistrust the intervention.

My other hope is that if we *did* track these side effects, we could learn something about our periods in general. Because it is very mysterious why and how these changes occur.

RACHEL

I want to talk more about mysterious changes.

There are so many stories of people losing their period after a loved one dies. I just heard a story about a young person who *got* her first period after her father died. And another story about someone who lost her period after her father died. Or someone who got her first period on her bat mitzvah. It just feels clear, from an anecdotal place, that these things are connected. Is there any science that can make sense of this?

ALICE

Feelings are a biological phenomenon; the more we learn in medicine and in science, the more that's clear.

We tend to discredit how important emotions are. But they're completely a part of our health—not just our mental health but our physical health as well.

Periods are controlled by hormones, which control our cycle. These hormonal fluctuations take place sequentially, both locally in the female reproductive system and in control centers in the brain.

Our *experiences* of the world and our *emotions* and *feelings* can actually impact that hormonal axis as well. An obvious example is stress—the stress hormone cortisol affects other hormones, including the hormones that control our periods. But that's just scratching the surface, because there are many other possible ways that emotions can influence our periods.

RACHEL

Hearing you talk, it makes me wonder why, during a doctor's checkup, they don't routinely ask about someone's menstrual cycle. It seems like such an effective way to understand someone's health holistically. And yet, I don't know if I've ever been asked.

ALICE

I think that's connected to the discomfort doctors feel around what they don't know. Some doctors are like, "I don't even know what's going on. I'm not going to get into that."

It's uncomfortable to not have the answers, especially on a topic that's already uncomfortable for many people to talk about openly. Clinicians *want* to be that confident fountain of knowledge who can explain everything that's going on. They want to be that source of reassurance, and the way they've been taught to do that is to have all the answers. But there are many things we don't have the answers for. And there is still a way to provide support and reassurance when we don't know everything, without avoiding the topic or oversimplifying.

I do think that's changing—we're learning to be more honest about what we don't know.

In terms of thinking about periods as an indicator of health, I want to stress that everyone's period is different.

What's important is what's normal for *you*. And if you deviate from what's normal for *your typical pattern*—and not everyone has one—that can tell you something.

One changed period is much less concerning than a chronic change in your period. Sometimes your body might shut down your period if it's not the "just right" conditions to sustain a pregnancy, which can be a *normal* part of your biology. But it can also be a sign of something else.

RACHEL

Just hearing you say all that is making me emotional. I really wish you had been my primary care provider.

ALICE

Everyone deserves to have a doctor who is willing to talk openly and honestly about both the knowns and unknowns.

Dr. Alice Lu-Culligan received her MD and PhD at Yale School of Medicine in the Department of Immunobiology, where she investigated the impact of antiviral immunity on pregnancy. She is a resident in pediatrics and an aspiring physician researcher with a passion for child development and women's health issues.

Feelings are biological phenomena.

A missing key was turned. A key that I didn't even know was missing.

My tante Nina's story no longer seemed like fate, or even like a dramatic story at all. It seemed physical, immediate, horrible. Our bodies are weather vanes for the world around us, and our blood lets us know.

My conversation with Alice brought back a distant memory of a time when my period mysteriously disappeared. After nine months, I finally went to the doctor. They put sucky cups all over my body and told me I would need to take hormones for the rest of my life.

I called my friend's mother, who is a doctor and also a Buddhist. She said, "Actually, your body may be working just fine. When the body is stressed, it sends signals not to reproduce. What you need to do now is tell your body that it's okay. That it's safe. Can you not work for a little while? Or, even more ideally, can you fall in love?"

Her prescription enraged and enchanted me in equal parts. Could I *just* fall in love? And how would that even affect my body?! A year went by. Nothing. No blood. And then, while I was buying a table off Craigslist from a stranger with a particularly lovely bookshelf, I felt something in my body. The morning after we slept together, I found myself screaming in the bathroom, "IT'S MY PERIOD!! YOU BROUGHT BACK MY PERIOD!!! FINALLY!!! THANK YOU!!!!!"

To publish this collection, I asked for various blessings. I talked again with my family. I wrote to writers who I'd been in touch with as a child.

Zannette, whose story is fourth in this book, had passed away since sharing her story. To find her family, I wrote to my mother, who wrote to a local poet, who wrote to another poet, who finally wrote to Zannette's son, Tchad. "Yes," he said. "You have my blessing to publish my mom's story. And what do you know, my daughter, who is Zannette's only biological granddaughter, just got her period. Shall I ask if she'd like to share her story?"

"Yes," I said, feeling a historic circle, much larger than me, come into its full shape.

Sofiya

I remember my hair being an absolute mess. It was probably because I hadn't showered for, like, four days. I don't really like showering or taking baths while I'm on my period. I find baths gross, because if you're sitting there for a while, you eventually start to see the little bloody skin clots floating around and that grosses me out to no end. I don't like showers on my period, either. My period makes it hard to stand up for a long time because my pelvic and uterus muscles are always aching and cramping. Alas, that day I had to take a shower because my mom invited me to go grocery shopping with her. And even though *I* know and *my parents* know that I don't take particularly great care of myself, people in the outside world don't need to know that.

Anyway, that day I was taking a shower. I really like hot showers, even when it's, like, 90 degrees outside. I also keep the curtain closed when I take showers, so I didn't notice how much hot steam was trapped inside this small, windowless, enclosed room until I opened said curtain. You can probably already tell where this is going . . .

As soon as I put one foot on the mat in front of the bathtub, my vision started to black out. I knew my body was overheated and that the combination with blood loss was making me very light-headed. I tried to get my body temperature back to normal. I didn't really know how much splashing cold water on my face would help, but I did it anyway. I cracked the bathroom door to get some of the cooler hallway air to circulate with the steaming-hot bathroom air. Now, mind you, I'm naked and soaking wet with blood dripping down my legs because I'm about to faint. When faced with such traumatic events, who has any time to put a tampon in? Anyway, I'm still naked in the bathroom, so I really only "cracked" the door open because I was worried about my parents walking down the hallway and seeing my bloody, naked body. Eventually I realized that splashing water on my face and drinking it wasn't quite cutting it with the whole "regulating Sofi's body temperature" thing, and I obviously wasn't feeling any better, so I grabbed a towel off the hook, wrapped it around my body, and left the bathroom in search of my mom. Luckily for me, she was just down the hall, and it was easy to call for her and grab her arm. It's actually kind of funny (or at least, I think it's funny), my mom thought I was trying to give her a hug, so she was pleasantly, not-so-pleasantly surprised when she saw me wrapped in a towel with my eyes half-lidded, water dripping from my hair, and blood running down my legs. But then I told her that it was hard to see and that I felt light-headed. She brought me over to her bed and made me lie down, even though I was soaking wet with bloody legs. To this day I still can't believe she did that for me.

Anyhoo, I lay there for a while until my head started to feel better and I could see again. After a good ten to fifteen minutes, I got up and went back to the bathroom, because I was very aware that there was still blood on the bathroom floor as well as on myself. I made it back, still wrapped in my towel, and started cleaning my legs off and putting on a pad so I wouldn't get any more blood anywhere. Even with my little "nap" on *my mom's bed*, I felt kind of light-headed. So like any girl who isn't feeling well, I lay down on my bathroom floor. Now, I can't explain to you why lying down on the bathroom floor is more comfortable than on a bed, but it just is. So there I was, lying on the bloody bathroom tile for half an hour or so until I started to feel better, for real this time. Once I "regained my strength," so to speak, I got up, got dressed, and brushed out my raggedy hair. Because even though *my parents* know and *I* know that I might not take the best care of myself, the outside world doesn't really need to know that.

Sofiya Moore is a thirteen-year-old girl who has stories to tell and likes telling them. She is a young person with modern perspectives about queerness and being biracial. She likes telling stories both fictional and autobiographical.

As someone who had been changed by my family's intimate histories, I also wanted to know what Sofiya felt sitting with her grandmother's words.

I was turning to Sofiya for some kind of wisdom. What do these stories do to us? How do they live in us? Why had I been listening to and gathering period stories all this time?

Here is what Sofiya wrote:

Sofiya Part II

The day that I was asked to write a piece reacting to my grandmother's story was actually her birthday. Even though she died before I really got to know her, it's wonderful to see her personality through her voice and writing. It was also powerful to hear my grandmother talk about her great-grandmother's experiences with slavery and her period. Although this story in particular was hard for me to stomach, I think stories like this one are so important to learn and hear about. The very thought of being sold to people and being used as breeding property for them makes me physically sick; my legs instinctively close, my stomach churns, and my throat closes up. It's horrible to think about that happening to a living, breathing human being.

It's funny to say, but I think the ending is my favorite part; it's so real and so true. Having your period really is a whole responsibility. It becomes this new thing that you have to think about, and take care of, and learn about, and feel about. It's such a big step into learning how to live with a uterus, and the road is really bumpy, and sometimes it's not so welcoming. But as you live through menstrual cycles in your life, you figure out how to own this "responsibility" and be proud of it. You eventually start to form this kind of "blood bond," so to speak, that will help you through it and provide support and words of wisdom. So reading the story my grandmother wrote really makes me feel not so alone on this bumpy and winding road.

I think we can end here, with Sofiya's words, which say so much about the spirit and the breath between your hands.

Though, of course, this isn't really the end, because this project is yours and mine as long as we want to listen.

A Note on Process

While gathering stories, I was guided by the following questions: What stories do I wish I had heard as a young person? What stories do I imagine I'll need to know in the future, which no one will tell me unless I ask? Clearly, those questions leave room for a lot of gaps. I was searching for something vital, though I wasn't quite sure what.

I tried so many other ways to make this book. At first I thought this book would be essays by writers and artists. Then I thought it should be oral histories gathered through word of mouth. And then I stopped trying to separate stories and contributors into categories, and decided to tell the story of what happened behind the scenes.

This book entailed decades of correspondence with contributors. There was writing followed by phone calls; writing followed by emails; writing followed by ten years of silence and then rewriting; writing that emerged from visiting classrooms, from visiting senior centers, and from asking people to talk with their loved ones, followed by collaborative editing. Each piece required its own process.

Contributions begin with someone's first name so that you can meet everyone sharing a story as a person, at eye level. Each contribution ends with a brief bio written by the contributor so that everyone can introduce themselves in and on the terms they view to be important.

With the exception of my family members, contributors received the majority of the advance from this book.

Acknowledgments

Thank you to each contributor for sharing your intimate histories with us.

Thank you to my teachers: Ellen Devine, Anne Fadiman, Fred Strebeigh, Sarah Ruhl, Alice Chung, Erin Courtney, Mac Wellman, Emily Mast, Rachel Bernsen, Elizabeth Visceglia, Julie Cho, and Erin Segal. You are all with me as I write and move through the world.

Thank you to my friends who are like sisters: Hope Kronman, Sarah Rosen, Cassie da Costa, Annie Woods, Sam Huber, Caitlin Ryan O'Connell, and, at all hours, Laurelin Kruse.

Bless you, Jerry, and the good people who support artists at the North American Cultural Lab, Brad Krumholz and Tracy Broyles, and everyone who first listened to a segment of this book out loud. Writing felt so much less lonely. Thank you to Mark Hernandez Motaghy, May Makki, Finn Jubak, Erica Harris, and Liz Brown for the insights and excellent energy.

Thank you to Claudia Romero, Ale Ballina, Ana Silvia Garza, Mariana Garza, María Perroni Garza, Jorge Ballina, Anna Barbierbi, Beatriz Olson, Wilhemina Jackson, Jace Liu, Ashley Galindo Lara, Diane Exavier, Meg Whiteford, Natalie Greene, Sallie Merkel, and Julia Sirna-Frest, whose stories, insights, and visions shaped this book. Thank you to Vikki

Law for connecting me to the writers you have built trust with over the years. Thank you to Katie Pichotta for your help many years ago that still reverberates into my life today.

Thank you to my family. To my aunts for the circle you've created around me. To my parents for your support. To my quietly visionary mother, Helen Kauder, thank you for opening the door to this world.

I am having trouble, as I tend to, with discrete categories. My friends are my teachers, and my teachers have become friends and collaborators. Susan Ginsburg, my agent, is also an honorary aunt.

Thank you to Jon Karp, from the very beginning. Thank you to Carina Guiterman and Rose Tomaszewska and Lashanda Anakwah and Catherine Bradshaw and Allyson Floridia and Lewelin Polanco, and everyone involved in the great labor of creating and sharing this book. Thank you for bringing your whole selves to this collaboration.

In the spirit of honoring my teenage self, thank you to the trees and all the natural resources involved in the fabrication of this book.

Thank you to the Lenape and the Quinnipiac peoples on whose land I'm grateful to live.

Thank you to my students and to all the artists I've worked alongside through 3 Hole Press. You are my teachers too.

To Carl. Thank you for holding me together during this sprawling project.

And thank you, forever, to Zoe, my sister.

Contributor Bios

212   **Katherine Agard** has more to say. She grew up in Trinidad and currently lives in the San Francisco Bay Area. Her first book, *of colour*, was longlisted for the 2021 OCM Bocas Prize for Caribbean Literature.

332   **Simran Ankolkar** is an artist and co-curator based in Mumbai observing, imagining, and archiving her surroundings. She likes to think of her work as embodying the notion of vessels—everything is a holding place for something.

127   **Hannah Bae** is a Korean American writer, journalist, and illustrator. She is the 2020 nonfiction winner of the Rona Jaffe Foundation Writers' Award, and she is working on a memoir about family estrangement and mental illness.

171   **Julianna Baldo** is an environmental advocate and high school student in Madison, Wisconsin. She has been working with the Youth Climate Action Team for two years.

280   **Pamela Beckford:** I am a free-going spirit. I like my friends. I live in Brooklyn. I am from Jamaica. And I enjoy walking in the early mornings. And I like baking, very much.

254   **Thaís Beltran** is a barista and proud member of the LGBTQ community. She enjoys exploring Chicago with close friends, DJing, and spending time with family.

25   **Nina Bentley** is a visual artist whose work often deals with women's social issues. Her sculpture *Corporate Executive*

Wife's Service Award Bracelet is part of the permanent collection of the New Britain Museum of American Art.

56 **Judy Blume** is the author of many books, including *Are You There God? It's Me, Margaret.*

242 **Mercedes Artime Bordas** is a Cuban immigrant who fled 1960s Cuba and the Castro regime as a little girl. She lives in San Juan, Puerto Rico.

223 **Agnes Borinsky** is a writer living in Los Angeles.

138 **C. C.** is an artist using text, image, performance, and sound to write poetry.

238 **Cassie da Costa** is a writer. She has an irregular newsletter of stories called *Mildly Yours* and covers film and television for *Vanity Fair*.

238 **Chilombo da Costa** is a public school educator and the mother of Cassie, Miranda, and Vanessa. Chilombo was born and raised in Lusaka, Zambia, and now lives in Pennsylvania with her husband, Chris.

161 **Maggie Di Sanza** (she/they) is the founder of Bleed Shamelessly and a grassroots organizer for reproductive justice and gender equity. Maggie has worked with Vote16 Madison, the Sexual and Reproductive Health Alliance of Dane County, and the Rape Crisis Center.

268 **Yehuda Duenyas** is an artist, an experiential director and designer, a creative director, an intimacy coordinator, and a father.

315 **Mindi Rose Englart** is a writer, artist, high school teacher, and, most recently, founder of the Single Mothers Discount Card.

36 **Enrique** represents the voices of several brothers and fathers in Mexico, gathered by theater director Claudia Romero.

61 **Trinidad Escobar** is a cartoonist from Milpitas, California. Her comics and poetry have been featured in literary journals and other publications, including *The Nib*, NPR, *The New Yorker*, and more. She is also the author of the forthcoming graphic novel *Of Sea and Venom* and the collection of Queer comics erotica *Arrive In My Hands*.

318 **Marian Evans** is an assistant professor in the Department of Public Health and Women's and Gender Studies at Southern Connecticut State University. She has taught a Women's Health and Women's Health Consciousness course for sixteen years. She is also a trained ob-gyn who brings period experiences and knowledge with her into the classroom, but her students have taught her so much more.

242 **Cristina Fernandez** is a performer, writer, and translator born and raised in La Isla Del Encanto to Cuban parents. Her work is often humorous, ritualistic, and in search of the transcendent.

156 **Madame Gandhi** is an LA-based artist and activist known for her uplifting, percussive electronic music and positive message about gender liberation and personal power. She has been listed as a Forbes 30 Under 30 in Music, and her 2020 TED Talk about conscious music consumption has been viewed over a million times.

302 **Nadia Gaskins** is a senior creative writer at Cooperative Arts and Humanities High School. Her interests include reading, writing, and crying to sad romance movies.

254 **Maria Gaspar** is an artist and mother hailing from Chicago's West Side. Her practice explores space, body, and power and has been supported by the United States Artists Fellowship, Creative Capital, Robert Rauschenberg Foundation, and Art for Justice Fund, among others.

305 **Axel Gay** is a junior in high school who has been working toward getting to know himself for years. He's recently come out as transgender to his friends and family.

 94 **Florence Given** is an illustrator, artist, and author of the *Sunday Times*–bestselling book *Women Don't Owe You Pretty*. Florence uses her bold slogans and '70s aesthetics to convey her messages and ideas about patriarchy, queerness, self-love, healing, personal growth, and acknowledging the intersections that affect each one of us differently in these areas. Florence is making it her mission to bring women together through her work and encourage us all to realize we are each the love of our own lives.

203 **Shira Grabelsky** is an artist and educator who loves being outside.

217 **Somáh Haaland** is a queer Indigenous artist and community organizer from the Pueblos of Laguna and Jemez in New Mexico who currently resides in New York City. They want every person reading this to feel seen and know that their life is sacred.

117 **Irena Haiduk's** written works and art are bonded by mutual making. To read more, seek out *Bon Ton Mais Non*, *Spells*, *Seductive Exacting Realism by Marcel Proust 12*, "Studio Feelings," and *All Classifications Will Lose Their Grip*.

100 **Fiona Hallinan** is an artist and early researcher, currently working on a doctoral project at LUCA School of Arts KU Leuven. She lives between Cork, Ireland, and Brussels, Belgium.

151 **Kwaneta Harris** is an incarcerated mother of three, living in solitary confinement with a wish to hug her children.

84 **Leah Hazard** is a Scotland-based midwife and the author of *The Father's Home Birth Handbook*, *Hard Pushed: A Midwife's Story*, and the forthcoming *Womb: The Inside Story of Where We All Began*.

148 **Zhi Kai Hoffman Vanderford** is a driven activist, eloquent poet, and motivated artist for human rights. He has been incarcerated for fifty-three years in the wrong body and for thirty-four years in prison. He is working on his master's degree with future hopes of helping LGBTQI youth navigate their lives.

263 **Henry Hoke** is the author of four books of fiction, memoir, and poetry. He cocreated and directs *Enter > text*, a living literary journal.

273 **Mara Hoplamazian** (they/them) is a writer from Chicago, Illinois.

144 **Elena House-Hay** is an incarcerated individual, artist, and writer who has found freedom in art and purpose in finally speaking up.

105 **Sarah Kane-Matete**, aka MamaSez, is of Filipino descent and resides in Tūranganui-a-Kiwa, Aotearoa. She is a *māmā* to three young children and a full-time artist in the mediums of painting and Indigenous tattoo in both *tā moko* and *tatak*. Sarah's work is inspired and guided by her journey of

coming home to self in identity and healing as an Indigenous woman with a strong *mana wāhine kaupapa*.

87   **Kubra Khademi**, born in 1989, is originally from Afghanistan and has lived in exile in Paris since 2015. She is a multidisciplinary artist and feminist whose works engage with the identity of women and refugee subjects.

235   **Barbara Bolanovich Kruse** is a lifetime Colorado resident and retired high school biology teacher. She hoped to spare her daughter from life's confusions but feels fortunate that they can share those experiences.

235   **Laurelin Kruse** is a writer living in Los Angeles.

273   **Kellyn Kusyk** (they/them) grew up in Virginia and is a writer and carpenter in Brooklyn.

179   **Monica Lennon** is an award-winning politician in Scotland who changed the law to introduce free universal access to period products. The world-leading legislation and campaign to end period poverty was pioneered by the Scottish Labour member of the Scottish Parliament in her first term, working with grassroots activists, trade unions, and equality organizations. The Period Products (Free Provision) (Scotland) Bill triumphed over many obstacles to achieve unanimous support in November 2020, making Scotland the first country in the world to make period products free to anyone who needs them. A former urban planner, Monica is an intersectional feminist, socialist, environmentalist, and mother to a teenage daughter.

19   **Zannette Eloise Lewis** was a dynamic source of wisdom and a beacon of inspiration for the many communities she steadfastly served during her too-short life. Organizations

that greatly benefited from her leadership include the Arts Council of Greater New Haven, Astrological Society of Connecticut, Inc., Connecticut Office of Higher Education, Episcopal Diocese of Connecticut, National Council of Negro Women, New Haven Museum and Historical Society, New Haven (CT) Chapter of The Links, Inc., and Yale Peabody Museum of Natural History. More than a decade after her passing, Zannette's spiritual light continues to shine over Connecticut and beyond.

47 **Ray Lipstein** works at *The New Yorker*.

249 **Mary Marge Locker** is a writer, researcher, and zine-maker. She grew up in Alabama and lives in New York.

249 **Lucy Locker Crosby** returned to the family farm in Alabama after thirty years as a business owner in the Mississippi Delta.

249 A thirty-year Tennessee educator, **Dr. Susan Locker Farris** also retired to the Alabama family farm.

334 **Dr. Alice Lu-Culligan** received her MD and PhD at Yale School of Medicine in the Department of Immunobiology, where she investigated the impact of antiviral immunity on pregnancy. She is a resident in pediatrics and an aspiring physician researcher with a passion for child development and women's health issues.

280 **Victoria Lynch:** I grew up in a big family, about fifteen people. My mother had ten kids, but lots of nieces and nephews and they were always there. Brothers and sisters, mother and granny . . . We weren't rich, but it was comfortable. We all lived together. We had enough to eat. We didn't have the luxuries that young people have, but we

were very happy. I left my island and came to the United States on a holiday. And I stayed here. When my time was up, I had grandkids here, and they said, "No, no, no, you stay here." So I said, "Okay, let me make a try." And I did get my paper and I stayed here. And I haven't regretted it because I have a beautiful apartment and I'm a citizen here now. I have no complaints. I have everything I need.

26   **Ma Xiao Ling** immigrated to the United States with her family in the aftermath of the Tiananmen Square massacre.

268   **Emily Mast** is an artist and a mother. Yehuda Duenyas and Emily are lovers, partners, and collaborators.

196   **Fatema Maswood** is a landscape architect, builder, and artist. They are first-generation Tunisian and Bangladeshi, and make work to dream about a future world remembered from traces. They find joy in working with soil and plants.

23   **Kica Matos** is a lawyer, social justice advocate, and organizer who lives in New Haven, Connecticut.

309   **Jordyn McBride** is currently a senior in college, studying marketing and management.

80   **Sam McCann** is a freelance stage manager working in live entertainment who loves animals.

71   **Michelle Memran** is a documentary filmmaker, illustrator, and writer. She divides her time between Brooklyn, New York, and Middletown, Connecticut. She is particularly interested in using creativity as a tool to move through illness. She also plays Ping-Pong.

345   **Sofiya Moore** is a thirteen-year-old girl who has stories to tell and likes telling them. She is a young person with

modern perspectives about queerness and being biracial. She likes telling stories both fictional and autobiographical.

75 **Daaimah Mubashshir** lives in Manhattan near a park. When she is not writing, her favorite pastime is to sit and people-watch with a friend.

105 **Ngahuia Murphy** is a researcher and author who comes from the Indigenous nations Ngāti Manawa, Ngāti Ruapani ki Waikaremoana, Ngāi Tūhoe, and Ngāti Kahungunu. Ngahuia's research specializes in reactivating Indigenous matrilineal ritual teachings.

286 **Salty Xi Jie Ng** is an artist from the tropical metropolis of Singapore. She cocreates semi-fictional paradigms for the real and imagined lives of humans within the poetics of the intimate vernacular. Often playing with social relations and structures, her work proposes everyday transcendence through humor, subversion, discomfort, a celebration of the eccentric, and a commitment to the deeply personal.

280 **Caitlin Ryan O'Connell** is a theater director and teacher living in Brooklyn who also likes baking and cooking for her family and friends.

263 **Melissa Oliver** is the mother of two sons. She grew up in Alabama and lives in Charlottesville, Virginia, where she works at the UVA Office for Equal Opportunity and Civil Rights.

41 **Claudia Pacheco** runs an alternative medicine clinic in Curitiba, Brazil. She studied Indigenous studies and ancient matriarchal cultures. She is a mother of two.

199 **Drew Pham** is a queer, transgender woman of Vietnamese

heritage whose writing meditates on legacies of violence, trauma, and memory. She is an educator whose philosophy centers on undoing racism and oppressive hegemonies through literature and writing. Though she cannot carry children, she is a mother to two beautiful, if spoiled, cats.

125 **Tamora Pierce** is the #1 *New York Times* bestselling author of over eighteen novels set in the fantasy realm of Tortall. Her writing has pushed the boundaries of fantasy and young adult novels to introduce readers to a rich world populated by strong, believable heroines. In 2013, she won the Margaret A. Edwards Award for her "significant and lasting contribution to young adult literature." Pierce lives in Syracuse, New York, and spends her free time herding feral cats.

161 **Amira Pierotti** (they/them) is a youth activist for transgender and gender-expansive rights, menstrual equity, and sexual assault survivor rights. They are a Lead Organizer with Bleed Shamelessly, a student facilitator of Game-Changers, a student representative on the Rape Crisis Center board of directors, and an advocate with a statewide coalition to end transphobia in Wisconsin.

206 **Mariana Roa Oliva** is a writer and criatura from Mexico City.

36 **Claudia Romero** is a theater maker. She directs, produces, writes, paints—whatever is needed. She is a theater believer.

122 **Sarah Rosen** is a writer and filmmaker.

66 **Sarah Ruhl** is a playwright, essayist, and poet living in Brooklyn. She is a two-time Pulitzer Prize finalist and

recipient of a MacArthur award. Her newest book is *Smile: The Story of a Face.*

111 **Alexis Sablone** is an artist, architect, and professional skateboarder living in Brooklyn, New York.

161 **Anika Sanyal** (she/her) is a youth organizer who is passionate about educational equity, reproductive justice, and youth enfranchisement. Anika was a Lead Organizer with Bleed Shamelessly between 2019 and 2021, and has worked with the Madison Metropolitan School District Student Senate, Vote16 Madison, and the Democratic Party of Wisconsin. Anika plans to study public policy at Swarthmore College.

187 **Gloria Steinem** is a writer, political activist, and feminist organizer. She was a founder of *New York* and *Ms.* magazines, and is the author of *The Truth Will Set You Free, But First It Will Piss You Off!*; *My Life on the Road*; *Moving Beyond Words*; *Revolution from Within*; and *Outrageous Acts and Everyday Rebellions.*

323 **Lily Grace Sutton** is a rising high school sophomore. Her hobby is keeping up with relationships. Her interests are animals and fashion.

286 **Tan Cha Boo** was born in and lives in Singapore. She is an exceptionally fit, fun-loving mahjong expert and fan of Teochew opera who cooks her food too sweet and salty.

286 **Teo Siew Lan** was born in and lived in Singapore. She abhorred mess, enjoyed working hard on her plants (especially the giant water jasmine bonsai she tended to for decades), shopping with her sister, and cooking treasured dishes for her family, such as the traditional Hokkien dumpling.

89 **Jennifer Thomas** is a mom of four adult daughters and three granddaughters, who are a joy and a pleasure. She is continually rewriting her personal script on womanhood through education and life experience.

209 **Una** writes and draws in a peaceful garden shed in Leeds, England. Her books include *Eve*, *Becoming Unbecoming*, *On Sanity: One Day in Two Lives*, and *Cree*.

329 **Odette Waks** is a ninety-one-year-old practicing psycho-analyst living in Paris. She describes herself as a doctor and psychiatrist who wants to understand "the source and the meaning of our symptoms, which is the subconscious."

91 **Tanaya Winder** is the author of *Words Like Love* and is a winner of the 2010 Orlando Prize in Poetry. Winder is currently working on her third poetry collection. She is Duckwater Shoshone, Pyramid Lake Paiute, and Southern Ute.

161 **Amy Yao** (she/they) is a teen activist who's involved with her school's Gender Equity Alliance. Amy is passionate about environmental, racial, and reproductive justice. She wants to make her community a better place for BIPOC queer youth. She is also an organizer with Bleed Shame-lessly.

311 **Piper Zschack** is a junior in high school and still a work in progress, but trying his best.

Permissions

Bassman, Nina, "Germany, 1942," in *My Little Red Book*, edited by Rachel Kauder Nalebuff. New York, NY: Twelve Books, 2010.

Anonymous high school excerpts. *My Little Red Book*.

Lewis, Zannette, "Loss and Gain of Responsibility, 1969," in *My Little Red Book*.

Matos, Kica, "Señorita, 1980," in *My Little Red Book*.

Bentley, Nina, "The Artist, 1968," in *My Little Red Book*.

Ma, Xiao Ling, "Chairman Mao's Period, 1967," in *My Little Red Book*.

Pacheco, Claudia, personal photograph.

Blume, Judy, "Clueless, 1952," in *My Little Red Book*.

Ruhl, Sarah, "Miscarriage," from *44 Poems for You* and excerpts from *Love Poems in Quarantine*. Copyright © 2020 and © 2022 by Sarah Ruhl. Reprinted with the permission of The Permissions Company, LLC on behalf of Copper Canyon Press, www.coppercanyonpress.org.

Pierce, Tamora, "Slippery in the Stairwell, 1965," in *My Little Red Book*.

Steinem, Gloria, "If Men Could Menstruate," in *Outrageous Acts and Everyday Rebellions*. New York, NY: Holt, Rinehart, and Winston, 1983. Provided with the permission of Gloria Steinem.

Reines, Ariana. "Purgatory." *Artforum*. December 29, 2020. https://www.artforum.com/slant/ariana-reines-s-full-moon-report-84769. Provided with the permission of Ariana Reines.

About the Author

Rachel Kauder Nalebuff is a writer working at the intersections of oral history, performance, and public health. She is the author of *Stages: On Dying, Working, and Feeling*; the co-editor of *The Feminist Utopia Project*; and the editor of the *New York Times* bestselling *My Little Red Book*. She teaches drama at senior centers and nonfiction writing at Yale University.